Essential Guide to LLMOps

Implementing effective strategies for Large Language Models
in deployment and continuous improvement

Ryan Doan

Essential Guide to LLMOps

Group Product Manager: Niranjan Naikwadi

Publishing Product Manager: Tejashwini R

Book Project Manager: Aparna Ravikumar Nair

Senior Editor: Gowri Rekha

Technical Editor: Rahul Limbachiya

Copy Editor: Safis Editing

Proofreader: Gowri Rekha

Indexer: Hemangini Bari

Production Designer: Nilesh Mohite

DevRel Marketing Coordinator: Vinishka Kalra

First published: July 2024

Production reference: 2050924

Published by Packt Publishing Ltd.

Grosvenor House

11 St Paul's Square

Birmingham

B3 1RB, UK

ISBN 978-1-83588-750-9

www.packtpub.com

To my fiance, Iris. Thank you for the love that you bring to my life each day.

– Ryan Doan

Contributors

About the author

Ryan Doan is a former ML engineer at Amazon and currently serves as the VP of technology at Semantic Health. He is also a private equity investor, focusing on **Software-as-a-Service SaaS**-based AI businesses, and the founder of MLExpert, a technical interview preparation course with over 60,000 students. Ryan has leveraged his technical expertise to develop machine learning models for diverse sectors, including trading firms, political campaigns, and government organizations. Most recently, he's spent three years at Semantic Health, which was acquired by AAPC in 2023. During this time, he led the development of **large language models** (LLM) applications that significantly enhanced revenue cycle management for hospitals in the US and Canada. In this book, Ryan shares what he learned from integrating language models and their operations into organizations, drawing on his broad experience to provide valuable insights into the effective use of these technologies.

I'm very grateful to my brothers and parents for their unwavering support and encouragement throughout all my ventures, no matter how challenging or outlandish they seem.

About the reviewer

Niharjyoti Sarangi is a machine learning scientist, with over a decade of experience in working on challenging problems in deep learning and building large-scale systems used by hundreds of millions of users. Niharjyoti's research interests span several areas in natural language processing and computer vision, including multi-modal large language models, user understanding, and deep reinforcement learning.

Currently, Niharjyoti works on solving complex user modeling challenges in the advertising space at Snap. Previously, he worked on driving user modeling for Microsoft Audience Network and developing natural language understanding models for Siri at Apple.

Table of Contents

Part 2: Tools and Strategies in LLMOps

3

Processing Data in LLMOps Tools   41

4

Developing Models via LLMOps   59

5

LLMOps Review and Compliance   85

Part 3: Advanced LLMOps Applications and Future Outlook

6

LLMOps Strategies for Inference, Serving, and Scalability   105

7

LLMOps Monitoring and Continuous Improvement 121

8

The Future of LLMOps and Emerging Technologies 141

Preface

Large language models (**LLMs**) stand as a pivotal advancement in AI, enhancing everything from chatbots to complex decision systems. As LLM applications grow, so does the need for specialized operational strategies, which we explore through the lens of **large language model operations** (**LLMOps**). This book aims to bridge the gap between traditional **machine learning operations** (**MLOps**) and the specialized requirements of LLMOps, focusing on the development, deployment, and management of these models.

Essential Guide to LLMOps introduces practices tailored to the unique challenges of language models, addressing technological implementations and stringent security and compliance standards. Through each chapter, this book covers the life cycle of LLMs across various industries, providing insights into data collection, model development, monitoring, compliance, and future directions. It is designed for a broad audience, from data scientists and AI researchers to business leaders, offering a comprehensive guide on navigating and leading in the complex landscape of large-scale language model applications.

Who this book is for

Primarily written for ML engineers, data scientists, and IT professionals, this book is ideal for those involved in the deployment, maintenance, and operational management of LLMs. It's particularly beneficial for professionals seeking to optimize LLM performance and integration and adhere to best practices and standards.

What this book covers

Chapter 1, Introduction to LLMs and LLMOps, compares LLMOps to traditional MLOps, highlighting the need for specialized approaches in AI development, deployment, and management. We will look at current trends in LLM applications across various industries, focusing on real-world uses, opportunities, and the importance of stringent security in LLM deployment. Core aspects of LLMOps, including model architecture, training methodologies, evaluation metrics, and deployment strategies, will be explored. We will also look at LLMOps in different applications and the intricacies of their operation and deployment.

Chapter 2, Reviewing LLMOps Components, discusses data collection, preprocessing, and how to ensure the dataset's quality and diversity. We will also look at developing and fine-tuning the model to ensure the right fit for the desired use case. This chapter also explores governance and review processes to ensure model accuracy, security, and reliability; inference, serving, and ensuring scalability to handle the demands of large-scale use and varied user interactions; and monitoring and continuous improvement to track performance and respond to user feedback.

Chapter 3, Processing Data in LLMOps Tools, looks at collecting, transforming, preparing, and automating data processes within LLMOps to enhance the efficiency and effectiveness of LLMs.

Chapter 4, Developing Models via LLMOps, covers creating, storing, and retrieving features; selecting foundation models; fine-tuning models; tuning hyperparameters; and automating model development to streamline model creation and deployment.

Chapter 5, LLMOps Review and Compliance, looks at how to evaluate LLM performance metrics offline, secure and govern models with LLMOps, ensure legal and regulatory compliance, and operationalize compliance and performance management.

Chapter 6, LLMOps Strategies for Inference, Serving, and Scalability, looks at inference strategies in LLMOps, optimizing model serving for performance, increasing model reliability, and scaling models cost-effectively.

Chapter 7, LLMOps Monitoring and Continuous Improvement, covers monitoring LLM fundamentals, reviewing monitoring tools and technologies, monitoring for metrics, learning from human feedback, incorporating continuous improvement, and synthesizing these elements into a cohesive strategy.

Chapter 8, The Future of LLMOps and Emerging Technologies, looks at identifying trends in LLM development, exploring emerging technologies in LLMOps, considering responsible AI, and developing talent and skill, as well as planning and risk management in the evolving field of LLMOps.

To get the most out of this book

The book assumes a foundational knowledge of ML, proficiency in Python programming, and a basic understanding of NLP. Familiarity with the challenges in MLOps and large-scale model management is recommended.

Software/hardware covered in the book	Operating system requirements
PyTorch	Linux
TensorFlow	
Airflow	
Azure	
GPU	

This book does not have a Github repository as the code is for illustrative purposes only. But if there are any noteworthy alterations or updates that will be important to the readers, we will be including the details here: `https://github.com/PacktPublishing/Essential-Guide-to-LLMOps`.

We do have other code bundles from our rich catalog of books and videos available at `https://github.com/PacktPublishing/`. Check them out!

Conventions used

There are a number of text conventions used throughout this book.

`Code in text`: Indicates code words in text, database table names, folder names, filenames, file extensions, pathnames, dummy URLs, user input, and Twitter handles. Here is an example: " Here, the given tokens are `["the", "recent", "advance", "ments", "in", ...]`.

The vocabulary is `{"the": 0, "recent": 1, "advance": 2, "ments": 3, "in": 4, ...}`"

A block of code is set as follows:

```
CREATE TABLE llm_token_data (
    token_id bigint,
    token text,
    frequency bigint,
    document_ids list<bigint>,
    PRIMARY KEY (token_id)
);
```

Bold: Indicates a new term, an important word, or words that you see onscreen. For instance, words in menus or dialog boxes appear in **bold**. Here is an example: "…and exploring the **Question Answering** benchmarks and datasets."

> **Tips or important notes**
> Appear like this.

Get in touch

Feedback from our readers is always welcome.

General feedback: If you have questions about any aspect of this book, email us at `customercare@packtpub.com` and mention the book title in the subject of your message.

Errata: Although we have taken every care to ensure the accuracy of our content, mistakes do happen. If you have found a mistake in this book, we would be grateful if you would report this to us. Please visit `www.packtpub.com/support/errata` and fill in the form.

Piracy: If you come across any illegal copies of our works in any form on the internet, we would be grateful if you would provide us with the location address or website name. Please contact us at `copyright@packt.com` with a link to the material.

If you are interested in becoming an author: If there is a topic that you have expertise in and you are interested in either writing or contributing to a book, please visit `authors.packtpub.com`.

Share Your Thoughts

Once you've read *Essential Guide to LLMOps*, we'd love to hear your thoughts! Scan the QR code below to go straight to the Amazon review page for this book and share your feedback.

https://packt.link/r/1-835-88751-1

Your review is important to us and the tech community and will help us make sure we're delivering excellent quality content.

Download a free PDF copy of this book

Thanks for purchasing this book!

Do you like to read on the go but are unable to carry your print books everywhere?

Is your eBook purchase not compatible with the device of your choice?

Don't worry, now with every Packt book you get a DRM-free PDF version of that book at no cost.

Read anywhere, any place, on any device. Search, copy, and paste code from your favorite technical books directly into your application.

The perks don't stop there, you can get exclusive access to discounts, newsletters, and great free content in your inbox daily

Follow these simple steps to get the benefits:

1. Scan the QR code or visit the link below

`https://packt.link/free-ebook/9781835887509`

2. Submit your proof of purchase
3. That's it! We'll send your free PDF and other benefits to your email directly

Part 1: Foundations of LLMOps

In the first section of this book, we review the foundational elements that constitute **large language model operations** (**LLMOps**). This part sets the stage for understanding the crucial aspects and underlying mechanics that support the efficient use and management of LLMs across various domains.

This part contains the following chapters:

- *Chapter 1, Introduction to LLMs and LLMOps*
- *Chapter 2, Reviewing LLMOps Components*

1

Introduction to LLMs and LLMOps

In this chapter, we'll examine the historical evolution of **natural language processing** (NLP) and the milestones leading to **large language models** (LLMs), gaining both a historical and future-oriented perspective on **large language model operations** (**LLMOps**). LLMOps refers to the processes, tools, and best practices that are adapted for the operational management of LLMs in a production environment. Our journey will explore how LLMs, through LLMOps, are revolutionizing various sectors by enabling complex tasks that once required human intelligence. We'll see how these models are embedded in digital applications, from virtual assistants to advanced media tools, becoming essential in our digital interactions.

In this chapter, we're going to cover the following topics:

- The evolution of NLP and LLMs
- Traditional MLOps versus LLMOps
- Trends in LLM integration
- The core concepts of LLMOps

The evolution of NLP and LLMs

NLP's inception can be traced back to the 1950s and 1960s, a period characterized by exploratory efforts and foundational research. During these early years, NLP was primarily driven by rule-based methods and statistical approaches, setting the stage for more complex developments in the decades to follow.

Rule-based NLP relied heavily on sets of handcrafted rules. These rules were designed by linguists and computer scientists to instruct computers on how to interpret and process language. For instance, early systems would break down text into components such as nouns, verbs, and adjectives, and then apply a series of predefined rules to analyze sentence structures and meanings. This approach was limited by its reliance on explicit rules, making the systems brittle and unable to understand the nuances of human language.

Around the same time, statistical methods introduced a new paradigm in NLP. Unlike rule-based systems, statistical NLP did not require hard-coded rules but instead utilized algorithms to analyze and learn from language data. This approach experimented with the idea that language could be understood and processed based on the probabilities of certain linguistic patterns or sequences occurring. One of the early applications of statistical methods in NLP was machine translation, exemplified by the work on the **Georgetown-IBM experiment** in the 1950s, which demonstrated the feasibility of using a computer to translate text from one language into another, albeit in a rudimentary form.

Despite these early strides, NLP faced significant challenges. One of the primary hurdles was the limited processing power. Early computers lacked the speed and memory capacities required to handle large volumes of language data or to run complex linguistic models. This significant bottleneck restricted the complexity of tasks that could be performed and the size of datasets that could be processed.

A final challenge was that early NLP algorithms were constrained by the computational and theoretical understandings of the time. They struggled to grasp the contextual and idiomatic aspects of language, which resulted in the output from these early systems sounding mechanical. This limited its applicability to real-world scenarios.

The rise of machine learning in NLP

Machine learning shifted the NLP paradigm from manually crafted rules to algorithms that learn linguistic patterns from vast amounts of data. This transition was driven by the recognition that the intricacies of language could be better captured through models that learn from real-world examples rather than predefined rules. The shift was gradual but steadily gained momentum as the effectiveness of machine learning models became increasingly evident.

Machine learning models, trained on large datasets, achieved higher accuracy rates in understanding and processing language than their rule-based predecessors. This increase in accuracy was not limited to specific tasks or datasets; machine learning models demonstrated a remarkable ability to generalize from the data they were trained on, making them applicable to a wide range of linguistic tasks.

Scalability was another area where machine learning had a significant impact. Unlike rule-based systems, which became increasingly complex and unwieldy as more rules were added, machine learning models could more easily scale up with the addition of data. This scalability was crucial in handling the ever-growing volume of digital text and speech data. It allowed for the development of NLP applications that could process and analyze large quantities of data efficiently, a capability that was unthinkable with rule-based systems.

Language modeling, the core purpose of many NLP approaches, involves predicting the probability of a sequence of words. This is fundamental for understanding and generating human language in many applications, such as **speech recognition**, **machine translation**, and **text prediction**.

N-gram models are one of the early techniques used in language modeling. An n-gram is a sequence of "n" words used to predict the next word in a sentence. For example, in a bigram (2-gram) model, the next word is predicted based on the previous one. Despite their simplicity, n-gram models were a staple in early NLP tasks due to their effectiveness in capturing the context of a sentence, though they are limited by the size of "n" and typically require large amounts of data to perform well.

As machine learning evolved, more sophisticated models, particularly those based on neural networks and deep learning, began to emerge. These models significantly advanced the capabilities of NLP by learning richer representations of text data. Neural networks, with their ability to learn complex patterns and dependencies in data, paved the way for deep learning models, which use layers of neural networks to process data in increasingly abstract forms. This led to revolutionary models in NLP such as **recurrent neural networks** (**RNNs**) and later, **Transformers**, which have significantly improved performance on many NLP tasks.

Deep learning revolution

The incorporation of deep learning into NLP marked a transformative era in AI's capability to understand and generate human language. The 2010s heralded the rise of neural network-based models, significantly altering the landscape of NLP and propelling an age of unparalleled linguistic comprehension and application by machines.

Deep learning, leveraging the architecture of artificial neural networks, introduced a radical shift in NLP. These multi-layered networks, inspired by the structure of the human brain, enabled models to autonomously discern complex patterns in language data. Deep learning's approach, learning directly from data without reliance on manually crafted features, proved pivotal. This advancement allowed models to grasp the intricacies and variations of human language, overcoming limitations faced by earlier systems.

The initial triumphs in neural networks for NLP were notable, especially with the development of word embeddings such as **Word2Vec** and **GloVe**. These embeddings revolutionized text representation, capturing semantic relationships in high-dimensional spaces and laying the foundation for advanced language processing.

A major breakthrough came with RNNs and **long short-term memory** (**LSTM**). RNNs, adept at processing sequential data, maintained an internal memory, using past outputs as inputs for subsequent operations. However, RNNs struggled with learning long-range dependencies due to the vanishing gradient problem. LSTMs, with their intricate internal structure, effectively retained information over longer periods, proving invaluable for various NLP tasks.

The impact of RNNs and LSTMs was particularly profound in machine translation. The introduction of **sequence-to-sequence (Seq2Seq)** learning, which employed an encoder-decoder framework, revolutionized this field. **Google's Neural Machine Translation system** exemplified this, translating entire sentences with contextual integrity, surpassing traditional phrase-based systems.

LSTMs also excelled in text generation, producing coherent, contextually relevant text sequences. This advancement enhanced automated content creation, ranging from journalism to creative writing. The text that was generated was not just syntactically accurate but also stylistically and thematically nuanced, often indistinguishable from human-authored content.

However, there remained some challenges with LSTMs. Firstly, LSTMs process data sequentially, which inherently limits their ability to utilize modern computing architectures, where parallel processing can significantly accelerate operations. This inefficiency became a critical hurdle as datasets and model complexity grew. Secondly, LSTMs often struggled to learn correlations between distant events in text due to the vanishing gradient problem. In LSTMs, as the sequence of data gets longer, the gradients (used in training the network) can become very small, essentially approaching zero. This occurs because errors in the LSTM's predictions are backpropagated through many layers of the network, multiplying these small errors together repeatedly. As a result, the weights in the network may receive minimal updates, losing their ability to contribute effectively to the model's learning process. This makes it difficult for LSTMs to maintain and utilize information over long text sequences, hindering their performance on tasks requiring an understanding of distant textual dependencies.

These limitations influenced the exploration and adoption of attention mechanisms in model architectures. Attention allows models to learn to focus on specific parts of the input data that are most relevant to the task at hand, effectively addressing both the parallelization issue by enabling more efficient computations and mitigating the impact of vanishing gradients by directly connecting distant data points in sequences. This led directly to the development of models such as Transformers, which rely on self-attention to process inputs in parallel and maintain a strong performance across longer sequences. Self-attention, a concept central to the Transformer model, is a mechanism that enables the model to weigh the importance of different words in a sentence, irrespective of their positional distance from each other. Unlike traditional models that process data sequentially, self-attention allows the model to process all words at once and to focus on the relevance of each word to others in the same input. This is achieved through a series of calculations that assign weights to these relationships, helping the model to better capture context and nuances in language.

The groundbreaking paper titled *Attention is All You Need*, released in 2017 by *Vaswani et al.*, introduced the Transformer model, which is built around this self-attention mechanism. This model marked a significant shift in how machine learning models are structured for processing language, moving away from the sequential processing of RNNs and LSTMs to a parallel architecture. The efficiency and effectiveness of Transformers in handling long sequences and their ability to maintain strong performance across these have made them highly influential in the field of natural language processing, leading to developments such as BERT, GPT, and other advanced models based on the Transformer architecture.

The birth of LLMs

The emergence of LLMs represents a significant milestone in the evolution of NLP. Characterized by their extensive scale and deep learning foundations, LLMs have transformed the landscape of AI's language capabilities. Central to this development are models such as **Bidirectional Encoder Representations from Transformers (BERT)** and the **Generative Pre-trained Transformer (GPT)** series, which have significantly influenced applications in translation, content generation, and beyond.

LLMs distinguish themselves through substantial neural network architectures and extensive training on vast datasets. These models predominantly utilize transformer architectures, known for parallel data processing and effective handling of long-range dependencies in text. This technological advancement underpins their effectiveness in understanding and generating language.

BERT, a groundbreaking model from Google, introduced a novel bidirectional training approach. By considering context from both sides of a word, BERT achieves a more nuanced understanding of language, enhancing performance in tasks such as sentiment analysis and question-answering. Its architecture has become a benchmark in the field, inspiring numerous adaptations and variations.

The GPT series, developed by **OpenAI**, takes a different approach with a left-to-right training model. These models excel in generating coherent, contextually appropriate text, showcasing advanced capabilities in text completion and conversation. The successive iterations of the GPT series have shown continuous improvements in scale and sophistication, significantly advancing AI's ability in human-like text generation.

In practical applications, LLMs have made substantial contributions. In machine translation, they offer enhanced fluency and accuracy, surpassing previous methods. In content generation, LLMs are capable of producing high-quality text for journalism, creative writing, and web content, often comparable to human-written text.

Moreover, LLMs have applications in sentiment analysis, document summarization, and automated question-answering systems. They are also increasingly used in specialized fields such as legal and medical text analysis, where their capability to process and interpret complex language is essential. Enhancing human-computer interaction, LLMs improve the sophistication and contextual awareness of chatbots and virtual assistants.

In essence, the development of LLMs has not only advanced the state of NLP but has also broadened the scope and depth of applications where **artificial intelligence (AI)** can effectively process and generate human language.

Current state and future directions

The current state of NLP and LLMs is characterized by rapid advancement and increasing integration into diverse applications. NLP, powered by LLMs, has achieved unprecedented levels of language understanding and generation, making significant strides in tasks such as machine translation, content creation, and conversational AI.

LLMs, such as the GPT series and BERT, represent the forefront of these advancements. These models, trained on extensive datasets and leveraging complex neural network architectures, have demonstrated a remarkable ability to comprehend and generate human-like text. They have been pivotal in enhancing machine translation's accuracy, creating more context-aware chatbots, and generating coherent, stylistically varied written content.

Looking to the future, the field is likely to witness continued growth in model sophistication and application diversity. Emerging trends include the integration of multimodal models capable of processing and correlating data from different sources such as text, images, and audio. There is also a growing emphasis on developing more efficient and environmentally sustainable models as current LLMs require significant computational resources.

Advancements in understanding and generating more nuanced aspects of language, such as humor, sarcasm, and cultural contexts, are also anticipated. This development will enhance the models' applicability in global and culturally diverse settings. Additionally, efforts are underway to improve models' ability to handle low-resource languages, expanding the reach of NLP technologies to a broader range of linguistic contexts.

However, deploying LLMs involves significant costs and challenges. The computational resources required for training and running these models are substantial, entailing high financial and environmental costs. Addressing these costs is crucial for making NLP technologies more accessible and sustainable.

Furthermore, ethical and fairness considerations in model training and outputs are increasingly coming to the forefront. Ensuring that LLMs are free from biases and that their use respects privacy and ethical standards is a growing concern and an area of active research and development.

Now, let's visit the operational requirements for LLMs in terms of LLMOps and how they differ from **machine learning operations (MLOps)**.

Traditional MLOps versus LLMOps

The field of AI has evolved significantly, leading to the specialization of MLOps and LLMOps. MLOps focuses on managing the life cycle of machine learning models, emphasizing integration, deployment, and monitoring, and addresses challenges in model versioning, data quality, and pipeline orchestration. LLMOps, however, deals specifically with the complexities of LLMs, such as extensive data and computational needs, and ethical considerations in training and output. While MLOps applies broadly to various machine learning models, LLMOps is tailored to the nuances of LLMs. Next, we'll explore the MLOps life cycle and what additional considerations are required for LLMOps.

Stages in the MLOps life cycle

MLOps is critical in transforming theoretical machine learning models into practical, real-world applications. Traditional MLOps involves deploying, monitoring, and maintaining these models within production environments, ensuring that they transition from conceptual frameworks to valuable, functional tools.

The MLOps life cycle can be split into a few key stages:

1. **Model development**: This initial stage involves creating and training machine learning models. Data scientists and engineers collaborate to select appropriate algorithms, train models on datasets, and fine-tune their parameters to ensure optimal performance.

2. **Testing**: Before a model is deployed, it undergoes rigorous testing to validate its accuracy, efficiency, and reliability. This phase is crucial to ensure that the model performs as expected when exposed to new data and in different scenarios.

3. **Deployment**: Once tested, the model is deployed into a production environment. This stage is challenging as it requires the model to be integrated into existing systems and ensure that it can handle real-time data at scale.

4. **Monitoring and maintenance**: Post-deployment, continuous monitoring is essential to ensure the model's performance does not degrade over time. This involves regular checks for accuracy, drifts in data, and other operational issues. Maintenance becomes crucial to updating models, retraining them with new data, and ensuring they remain effective and relevant.

Specific challenges and methodologies in LLMOps

LLMOps distinctively stands out from traditional machine learning workflows due to its complexity. The management and operation of LLMs involve advanced techniques and methodologies that are essential for harnessing their full potential.

The additional steps concerning the LLMOps life cycle are as follows:

- **Training corpus gathering**: This initial stage involves creating a corpus (>1 trillion) of linguistic tokens. These tokens are character sequences derived from raw textual data, including books, websites, articles, and social media. Machine learning scientists and engineers collaborate to ensure the right breadth, depth, and format is represented.

- **Foundation model pre-training**: An untrained model such as GPT is then chosen to apply the training tokens. This involves assigning IDs to each unique token and training the autoregressive GPT model to predict subsequent token IDs based on previously seen token sequences. A test set is held out to adjust the model's hyperparameters to ensure optimal performance and model convergence. This process can require millions of USD in compute power, so many open source models have already undergone this training process.

- **Foundation model fine-tuning:** Once trained, the model needs to be trained more on examples that explicitly apply to a desired use case. For example, assuming we need a GPT model to transform unstructured text in JSON format, we need to create a dataset of several thousand pairs containing unstructured text and the respective JSON format. These examples will be used to further train the foundation model.

Trends in LLM integration

LLMs have evolved from technological novelties to become essential components in various industries, reshaping standard practices and setting new benchmarks for efficiency and innovation. This section examines how LLMs are integrated across different sectors, focusing on current trends and applications, and contemplating their future implications and possibilities.

Integration of LLMs across industries

The integration of LLMs across industries has enhanced operational efficiency and innovation. These sectors leverage the capabilities of LLMs to meet specific challenges.

Healthcare

LLMs in healthcare parse and interpret large volumes of medical texts, research papers, and patient data. They aid medical professionals in diagnosing diseases by analyzing symptoms and medical histories, thus contributing to informed decision-making. Additionally, LLMs support the development of personalized medicine, tailoring treatment plans based on individual patient data.

Finance

LLMs scrutinize financial reports, market trends, and consumer data, aiding in risk assessment and fraud detection. They analyze transactional data to spot patterns that may indicate fraudulent activity, thereby enhancing risk mitigation. LLMs also automate customer interactions and guide customers to appropriate financial advisors for personalized advice.

Education

LLMs transform education by providing interactive question-and-answer interfaces, allowing students to explore topics at their own pace and interest. They also assist educators by grading assignments and offering feedback, reducing their workload.

Law

LLMs expedite the analysis of legal documents, case laws, and contracts. They facilitate legal research by rapidly processing extensive legal texts, aiding lawyers in case preparation. LLMs further assist in drafting legal documents, ensuring compliance, and minimizing manual effort.

Customer service

Customer service has evolved with the advent of LLM-driven chatbots and virtual assistants. These tools efficiently handle customer queries, reducing the need for human intervention in most cases. This not only streamlines customer service operations but also reduces associated costs.

Content generation

LLMs, including multi-modal variants, are employed in content generation for articles, blogs, and marketing materials. They enable rapid content prototyping and creation, significantly reducing the time and resources traditionally required for content development.

Current trends and examples of LLM applications

LLMs are extensively applied across various industries, becoming a ubiquitous element in numerous applications. They're transforming AI applications in a broad range of areas, including content generation and conversational AI.

Text-to-text applications

LLMs are crucial in text-to-text tasks within NLP, specifically in summarization, translation, and question-answering. For summarization, LLMs utilize evaluation methods such as the **Recall-Oriented Understudy for Gisting Evaluation (ROUGE) Score** and **BLEU metrics**, enabling businesses to efficiently condense lengthy documents, thus facilitating quicker decision-making. In translation, LLMs trained on comprehensive parallel corpora and assessed using **Metric for Evaluation of Translation with Explicit Ordering (METEOR) metrics**, effectively overcoming language barriers, which is essential for international business operations. In question/answering, LLMs' context-aware algorithms provide precise, real-time responses, enhancing business support systems.

Code generation and bug fixing

LLMs, trained on vast coding databases, are instrumental in predicting code snippets, significantly speeding up software development. Employing structures such as abstract syntax trees ensures accuracy, and for bug fixing, integration with static code analysis tools helps in identifying and correcting code vulnerabilities. This enhances both the efficiency and security of business software solutions.

Sentiment analysis

In sentiment analysis, LLMs, part of the **natural language understanding** (NLU) subset, adeptly identify sentiment indicators in text. Using advanced neural networks and tools, such as **TextBlob** and **VADER**, LLMs facilitate the integration of real-time sentiment analysis into **customer relationship management** (CRM) systems, enabling more nuanced customer interactions.

Data structuring

LLMs analyze and interpret raw text data, extracting key information and organizing it into structured schemas such as JSON or XML. This capability is particularly useful for processing data from diverse sources such as social media, customer feedback, or unstructured documents. The LLMs discern relevant data points, such as names, dates, and other specifics, and categorize these elements into structured, machine-readable formats.

Future outlook and potential developments

The future outlook and potential developments for LLMs indicate significant advancements in areas such as large multi-modal models, deployment on edge computing, and the emergence of open source alternatives to commercial models.

Large multi-modal models

Future developments in LLMs are increasingly focusing on multi-modal models that can process and integrate different types of data, such as text, images, and audio. These models aim to understand and generate information in a way that mirrors human cognitive abilities more closely. By integrating various data types, multi-modal LLMs can provide more comprehensive and nuanced responses, enhancing applications in areas such as AI assistants, content creation, and automated analysis systems.

LLMs on edge computing

The deployment of LLMs on edge computing platforms represents a significant shift. Traditionally, the computational demands of LLMs necessitate cloud-based infrastructure. However, advancements in edge computing technology are expected to allow more processing to be done locally on devices. This shift can lead to reduced latency, enhanced privacy, and lower bandwidth usage, making LLMs more accessible and practical for real-time applications in remote or network-constrained environments.

Open source equivalent to commercial offerings

There is a growing trend toward open source equivalents of commercial LLMs. These open source models offer several benefits, including increased transparency, customizability, and broader accessibility for researchers and smaller enterprises. As the open source community continues to grow, these models will likely reach parity with commercial offerings in terms of capabilities, further democratizing access to advanced NLP technology. This can spur innovation and application development as more users gain access to high-quality LLMs without the constraints of commercial licensing.

Core concepts of LLMOps

LLMOps takes the foundational principles of traditional MLOps and adapts them to the unique context of managing and deploying large-scale language models. This section dives into the core concepts and terminology unique to LLMOps, exploring how they differ from and build upon traditional MLOps practices.

Key LLMOps-specific terminology

Understanding LLMOps requires familiarity with certain specific terms and concepts that are referenced in the field:

- **GPT**: A specific type of Transformer model known for its effectiveness in generating human-like text, showcasing the capabilities of modern LLMs.

- **Transformer architectures**: Advanced model structures key to modern LLMs, known for their self-attention mechanisms and parallel processing capabilities.

- **Attention mechanisms**: Part of Transformer architectures, these mechanisms help LLMs focus on relevant parts of the input data for better language processing.

- **Tokenization**: The process of breaking down text into **smaller units** (**tokens**) for neural network processing, crucial in understanding language nuances in LLMs.

- **Context windows**: The span of text an LLM considers at any one time, impacting its ability to generate contextually relevant and coherent language.

- **Pre-training**: The initial phase of training an LLM on large, diverse datasets to develop a broad understanding of language before fine-tuning.

- **Fine-tuning**: The process of adapting a pre-trained LLM to specific tasks or domains by training on task-specific datasets.

- **Language model evaluation metrics**: Specific metrics used to assess the performance of LLMs, such as BLEU for translation or ROUGE for text summarization.

Model architecture

Transformers mark a shift from traditional machine learning architectures in both complexity and functionality. These models are specifically designed to meet the distinct challenges associated with processing and generating human language. This distinguishes LLMs from architectures used in other machine learning tasks.

Advanced architectures in LLMs

Transformers have transformed approaches to language tasks in machine learning. Differing from traditional architectures such as RNNs and LSTMs, which process data sequentially, Transformers employ self-attention mechanisms for parallel data processing. This allows for comprehensive consideration of word context within sentences, enhancing language understanding and generation.

Unique design considerations for LLMs

A key focus in LLMs is managing long data sequences. Traditional models falter with long-term dependencies, losing the relevance of information over extended sequences. Transformers counter this through attention mechanisms, enabling the model to assess the significance of different input data sections, irrespective of their sequential position.

Attention mechanisms allow the model to selectively concentrate on various parts of the input, identifying the most pertinent elements for specific tasks. This feature is used in applications such as language translation, where context and meaning can significantly fluctuate within a sentence.

Challenges and innovations in scaling up LLM architectures

Scaling LLM architectures poses challenges that are different from those in typical MLOps models. The immense size of LLMs, often encompassing billions of parameters, requires extensive computational resources for both training and inference. This has prompted innovations in distributed computing and model parallelism, distributing the model across multiple GPUs or TPUs to handle the computational demands. Innovations in data caching, model sharding, and optimization algorithms have been essential for training these large models effectively.

The development and deployment of LLMs also highlight concerns regarding the environmental impact of such extensive computations. Consequently, there is an increasing focus on enhancing model energy efficiency through architectural optimizations, improvements in the efficiency of the supporting hardware, and offloading computation to edge devices.

Pre-training and fine-tuning in LLMOps

The processes of pre-training and fine-tuning LLMs exhibit distinct characteristics compared to conventional MLOps, particularly in terms of scale, task complexity, and the intricacies of model optimization.

The pre-training phase in LLMOps

Pre-training in LLMOps involves training LLMs on extensive, generalized datasets to develop a foundational language model. This phase uses algorithms capable of processing vast amounts of unstructured text data, typically leveraging advanced neural network architectures such as Transformers. The pre-training process aims to equip LLMs with a comprehensive understanding of linguistic patterns, syntax, and semantics across diverse text sources. Unlike traditional machine learning models, which might focus on narrow datasets, LLMs during pre-training ingest a much wider array of text, often including entire corpora such as web pages, books, and articles, to develop a robust baseline language model.

The fine-tuning phase in LLMOps

Post pre-training, fine-tuning customizes LLMs to specific tasks or domains. This phase involves training the model further on specialized datasets that are smaller yet highly relevant to the intended application, such as *domain-specific corpora* for legal or medical language processing, or *targeted datasets* for applications such as sentiment analysis or machine translation. The fine-tuning process adjusts the weights of the pre-trained model to enhance its performance on these specific tasks, often requiring iterations to balance the model's general language understanding with its specialized task performance.

Challenges in LLMOps training

One of the primary challenges in LLMOps training is managing the sheer volume and variety of training data. Ensuring representativeness and diversity in the training datasets is crucial to avoid biases and enhance the model's versatility across linguistic contexts. This often requires careful curation and augmentation of datasets to cover underrepresented languages or dialects.

Bias mitigation is another critical concern as LLMs are susceptible to adopting biases present in their training data. This necessitates sophisticated techniques for bias detection and mitigation, such as differential privacy methods or adversarial training approaches, to ensure the outputs of the models are fair and unbiased.

Furthermore, preventing overfitting is paramount, especially considering the complexity and size of LLMs. Overfitting can lead to models that are overly specialized to the training data, reducing their efficacy on real-world, unseen data. Techniques such as dropout, layer normalization, and careful hyperparameter tuning are employed to address this challenge. Additionally, performance metrics monitoring, including perplexity measurements for language models and F1 scores for specific tasks, is essential to evaluate and maintain the models' effectiveness.

Evaluation metrics and methods in LLMOps

The evaluation of LLMs in LLMOps is a detailed and intricate process that's distinct from traditional MLOps evaluation methods. This evaluation is integral to determining the efficacy and dependability of LLMs in language-related tasks.

LLMOps-specific evaluation metrics and methods

In LLMOps, specific metrics and methods are utilized to gauge LLM performance, especially in language generation tasks. Metrics such as ROUGE and METEOR are employed. ROUGE is used predominantly for text summarization evaluation, measuring the n-gram overlap between the generated summary and reference summaries. METEOR extends beyond mere overlap by including synonym matching and stemming, offering a more comprehensive assessment of machine translation.

These metrics aim to quantify language output quality while considering aspects such as fluency, informativeness, and conformity to reference texts, providing measurable indicators of the LLMs' language generation alignment with expected human language outcomes.

Challenges in evaluating LLMs

Evaluating LLMs involves challenges, particularly regarding subjective language aspects such as coherence, creativity, and contextual appropriateness. Assessing coherence involves determining logical consistency and structure in the output. Creativity evaluation examines the model's capacity for novel and engaging content creation, while contextual appropriateness assesses the model's ability to recognize and respond suitably to various conversational nuances.

Quantifying these subjective aspects is complex, often exceeding the capabilities of automated metrics, due to the nuanced and intricate nature of human language.

The importance of human-in-the-loop evaluations

Human-in-the-loop evaluations are crucial in LLMOps due to the human-centric nature of language models. This approach incorporates human judgment in the evaluation process, offering a comprehensive and subjective analysis of the model's output.

Human evaluators can discern aspects such as language naturalness, conversational appropriateness, and content creativity, which automated metrics might overlook. They also aid in identifying biases or errors not immediately apparent through automated evaluations.

Integrating human feedback is essential for the continuous refinement of LLMs, ensuring their outputs adhere to human standards and expectations. This approach is particularly important in applications where LLMs interact with users or generate content mirroring human expression and emotion.

LLMOps workflow overview

LLMOps represent the culmination of advanced machine learning practices tailored specifically for LLMs. It encapsulates an end-to-end process that ensures these models are not only built with the highest level of technical expertise but are also deployed and managed in ways that maximize their utility and adhere to ethical standards.

Step-by-step overview

This LLMOps life cycle encompasses several distinct phases, each critical to the successful deployment and operation of LLMs.

Data selection and preparation

This forms the basis for the performance and effectiveness of LLMs. Datasets must be expansive to ensure broad coverage, diverse to capture various linguistic nuances, and inclusive to reflect a wide array of language use cases. Such well-rounded datasets are a key factor for their functionality and accuracy.

Data quality directly impacts the model's performance. Rigorous data cleaning and preprocessing are essential, entailing the elimination of inconsistencies, errors, and extraneous information. This approach to data preparation bolsters the model's learning efficiency and increases the likelihood that the resulting outputs are applicable in practical scenarios.

Foundation model selection

Selecting the appropriate foundational model greatly affects the overall effectiveness and relevance of the outputs. This selection demands a nuanced consideration of various factors to align with the project's specific goals and constraints. Considerations include the model's intended application, the range and complexity of languages it must encompass, and its intrinsic learning capabilities.

Pre-training and fine-tuning

Pre-training on diverse datasets is instrumental in providing the model with an understanding of natural language. The aim is to endow the model with a wide-ranging understanding of language nuances. Exposure to diverse linguistic styles, contexts, and structures enables the model to acquire a versatile and in-depth grasp of language, a vital aspect of its applicability across various tasks.

Post pre-training, LLMs undergo fine-tuning, where they're specifically tailored and refined. This stage involves training the models on datasets particular to their intended tasks or operational domains. Fine-tuning transforms a generalist language model into a task-specific specialist, enhancing its capability to execute designated tasks such as translation, content generation, or sentiment analysis with greater precision and relevance. This progression from broad learning to targeted refinement is essential for LLMs to achieve robust language processing proficiency, accuracy, and efficacy in specific applications.

Scalable deployment

The deployment of LLMs necessitates strategic planning due to their substantial size and complexity. This involves the use of distributed computing and cloud-based environments, which offer the required computational power and scalability. Such an approach facilitates the efficient allocation of computational tasks, enabling the models to process extensive datasets and execute intricate language functions without straining any single system excessively.

Deploying LLMs also demands a focus on ensuring their accessibility and prompt responsiveness in diverse application scenarios. These models must maintain high operational efficiency and rapid response times, regardless of whether they're used for individual interactions or in large-scale enterprise applications. Achieving this level of responsiveness involves thorough planning and optimization of both the models and their adjacent infrastructure. Key strategies include refining the model's architecture for accelerated inference, employing effective data caching methods, and applying load balancing to manage user requests efficiently. The objective is to establish a deployment environment where LLMs consistently deliver optimal performance and offer users swift and precise language processing capabilities across various applications.

Continuous monitoring and updating

Continuous performance monitoring is crucial to ensure LLMs maintain their efficacy. This involves regularly assessing metrics such as accuracy, response time, and error rates to ensure the model's outputs remain consistent and dependable. Monitoring is key in identifying issues such as model drift or degradation, which may arise from evolving data patterns or user interactions. Diligently tracking these indicators enables LLMOps teams to sustain optimal LLM functioning, ensuring precise and pertinent user responses.

Adaptive updating addresses the evolving nature of language and communication. As language is dynamic and new data constantly emerges, LLMs require regular updates to stay current. This process often involves retraining or fine-tuning the models with recent data, encompassing new vocabulary, linguistic patterns, or shifts in language use. These updates help the models stay relevant in terms of contemporary language use and trends.

Security considerations

Addressing security issues such as training data leakage, governance, compliance, and risk mitigation is vital. These factors are essential for preserving the integrity of the models and user trust.

Training data leakage poses a significant risk in LLMOps. Steps must be taken to prevent sensitive information in training datasets from unintentionally becoming part of the model's output. Leakage risks privacy violations and compromises both user confidentiality and model integrity. To prevent this, stringent vetting and anonymization of training data are required, alongside strict data handling protocols to prevent unintended disclosures.

Governance and compliance are vital in LLMOps. Models must be developed and operated within legal data protection frameworks to ensure they adhere to regulations such as the **General Data Protection Regulation (GDPR)** in Europe and other regional laws. Effective governance involves clear policies for data usage, model training, and deployment, ensuring transparency and accountability in all operations.

Mitigating security risks associated with LLM deployment and use is another key concern. As LLMs integrate into various systems, they become potential targets for attack. Robust security measures, including strong access controls, data encryption, and consistent monitoring of model usage, are imperative for preventing unauthorized access and misuse.

Comprehensive approach in LLMOps

LLMOps demands a multifaceted approach that merges technical skills with practical considerations. This requires ensuring that models are technically proficient and perform optimally while being performant and cost-effective. Data privacy, security, and cost considerations are essential components of the LLMOps workflow.

Real-world example

This workflow can be seen in **ACS's automated customer service** offering, which required their foundation model to be pre-trained to avoid unexpected customer experiences.

Data collection and pre-processing

ACS began by aggregating a vast corpus of customer service transcripts, email exchanges, and social media interactions. This data underwent pre-processing, where irrelevant information was filtered out, such as prices and **personally identifiable information** (PII). About 1T tokens were created for pre-training.

Foundation model selection

ACS decided to implement and use Llama 2 as the foundation model by replicating the published paper. ACS implemented the model themselves so that they could pre-train it from scratch. This allowed ACS to control the knowledge and scope of the model.

Pre-training phase

Pre-training required about 100,000 hours of A100 compute, which equated to about $150,000. In comparison, the official release of Llama 2 was trained on 2T tokens for about a quarter of a million dollars.

Fine-tuning phase

Three snapshots of the pre-trained model were then each separately fine-tuned based on their desired customer service application: email exchanges, social media interactions, and voice transcripts.

Model deployment

Once fine-tuned, the models were deployed via Azure AI and integrated as part of the company's customer service platform. This deployment included integration with the company's existing CRM systems for a seamless user experience.

Continuous monitoring and updating

The LLMOps team continuously monitors the model's performance, tracking metrics such as accuracy, response time, and cost. They also watch for model drift or degradation in performance. The model is periodically updated with new data so that it can keep up with evolving domain and customer service needs. These updates involve re-training portions of the model with recent data to maintain its relevance and accuracy.

Security and compliance

The organization ensures strict adherence to security protocols. Data encryption, access controls, and regular security audits are conducted to safeguard the model and the data it processes. Compliance with legal standards and ethical guidelines is consistently monitored and maintained.

Summary

This chapter shed light on the intricate dynamics of language models in the realm of AI and also laid a robust foundation for understanding the complex world of LLMOps.

First, we looked into the historical progression of NLP, reviewing its evolution from rule-based systems to the advent of transformative LLMs. This journey highlighted the significant milestones and the technological advancements that have led to the development of sophisticated models such as GPT and Llama 2.

Next, we underscored the distinct challenges intrinsic to LLMOps, contrasting them with traditional MLOps. The scale, complexity, and unique requirements of LLMs require a specialized approach, differing significantly from conventional machine learning models.

After, we observed how LLMs are increasingly being integrated across various industries, reshaping the landscape of digital interaction and content generation. This integration signifies the growing influence and versatility of LLMs in practical applications.

Finally, this chapter introduced key concepts such as Transformer architectures, tokenization, context windows, and the importance of model scalability and evaluation, providing a deeper understanding of the technicalities involved in LLMOps.

A step-by-step walk-through of the LLMOps workflow, from model selection and design to deployment and monitoring, offered a comprehensive view of the processes involved in managing LLMs. This overview highlighted the complexity of deploying and maintaining these language models. In the next chapter, we will review LLMOps components.

2

Reviewing LLMOps Components

In this chapter, we'll dive into the components of LLMOps and how each piece enhances the efficiency, quality, and performance of the underlying LLMs. This chapter serves as a high-level overview that subsequent chapters will explore in depth. Our focus will be on the following areas and their impact:

- Data collection and preparation
- Model pre-training and fine-tuning
- Governance and review
- Inference, serving and scalability
- Monitoring
- Continuous improvement

Data collection and preparation

Data collection and preparation form the backbone of **large language model** (**LLM**) training and efficiency. This phase involves gathering, processing, and storing data in a manner that makes it most useful for training LLMs.

Data collection

Data collection for LLM training typically involves sourcing from a variety of public datasets that are rich in language diversity. These datasets include the following:

- **Web text**: Data scraped from websites, encompassing a wide range of topics and styles
- **Books and publications**: Texts from books, especially those in the public domain, provide a classic and varied literary perspective

- **Social media feeds**: Platforms such as Twitter or Reddit offer insights into colloquial and current language usage

- **News articles**: Datasets from news websites present formal and contemporary language

Here's an example of what a web scraper may obtain from a news site in JSON form:

```
{
  "url": "http://example-news-website.com/article1",
  "content": "<!DOCTYPE html><html><head><title>AIAdvancements</
title></head><body><h1>The Recent Advancements in AI</h1><p>The recent
advancements in AI have been rem...",
  "date_published": "2021-07-01",
  "author": "John Doe"
}
```

The preceding JSON snippet shows the content and associated metadata for a particular website. We'll use the content in this JSON structure in the next step of processing.

Processing raw text

The raw text inside the content of the JSON undergoes several processing steps:

1. **Cleaning**: Removing irrelevant content such as HTML tags, ads, or navigational elements:

    ```
    {
      "content": "The recent advancements in AI have been
    remarkable. With new applications emerging across different
    sectors.."
    }
    ```

2. **Normalization**: Standardizing text, such as converting it into lowercase, to reduce variations:

    ```
    {
      "content": "the recent advancements in artificial intelligence
    have been remarkable. With new applications emerging across
    different sectors.."
    }
    ```

3. **Sentence segmentation**: Breaking text into individual sentences for better context understanding:

    ```
    {
      "content": ["the recent advancements in artificial
    intelligence have been remarkable."], ["With new applications
    emerging across different sectors.."]
    }
    ```

4. **De-duplication**: Eliminating repeated content to ensure data quality:

```
["the recent advancements in artificial intelligence have been
remarkable."], ["With new applications emerging across different
sectors.."]
```

These processing steps turn the raw text into something that we can tokenize. We'll cover the tokenization process in the next section.

Tokenization

Tokenization is a critical step where text is broken down into smaller units called tokens. These tokens can be words, subwords, or characters, and the choice of tokenization level has significant implications for the model's design and performance.

One of the main reasons to consider different tokenization strategies, such as subword tokenization, relates to vocabulary size. A large vocabulary can lead to increased memory requirements and slower processing speeds, whereas a small vocabulary might not be sufficient to capture the nuances of the language effectively.

Using subword tokens strikes a balance between having too large a vocabulary and not capturing enough linguistic details. Subword tokenization involves splitting words into smaller, meaningful units. This method allows the model to handle unknown words better as it can decompose them into known subunits. For instance, the word *"unbreakable"* could be split into *"un-," "break,"* and *"-able,"* which are likely to appear in other contexts within the training data.

Subword tokenization reduces the problem of **out-of-vocabulary** (**OOV**) words, which are not seen during training and can cause issues during model inference. By breaking words into common subwords, the model can assemble unseen words from these known pieces, enhancing its ability to generalize and understand new inputs. This approach also allows for more efficient use of the model's vocabulary, enabling it to learn more from less data and reducing the number of parameters it needs to train.

Let's look at an example of tokenization. Say we have `"the recent advancements in artificial intelligence have been remarkable."` as input text. In this case, the tokens would be `["the", "recent", "advance", "ments", "in", ...]`.

Token ID assignment

After the initial tokenization, each unique token is assigned a distinct identifier, often referred to as a token ID. First, a vocabulary is created from the tokens. This vocabulary is essentially a list or dictionary where each unique token is listed.

Each token in the vocabulary is then assigned a unique numerical ID. These IDs are usually sequential numbers starting from a specific number, often 0 or 1.

Here, the given tokens are `["the", "recent", "advance", "ments", "in", ...]`.

The vocabulary is `{"the": 0, "recent": 1, "advance": 2, "ments": 3, "in": 4, ...}`

In machine learning, and particularly in NLP, models process numerical data. By converting tokens into unique IDs, textual data is transformed into a numerical format that can be fed into neural networks.

Using token IDs, instead of the actual text, makes data processing more efficient. Numerical operations are generally faster and more optimized in computational environments. Despite this conversion to numerical IDs, the semantic and syntactic meaning embedded in the original text is preserved, which is crucial for the model to learn and make predictions.

Storing token ID mappings

The mappings between tokens and their IDs are stored in a data structure, often referred to as the tokenizer model or vocabulary file. This file is used during model training and when processing new text for predictions. The tokenizer model can be stored in various formats, such as JSON or a binary file, depending on the requirements and the specific framework or library being used. When the LLM processes text, it refers to this tokenizer model to convert the input text into a sequence of token IDs. The model then uses these sequences for training or inference tasks.

Dataset storage and database management systems (DBMSs)

Once processed, the dataset is stored in a format and structure suitable for model training. The storage schema typically involves a tabular format with fields for different attributes of the text (for example, the content, source, and date). Let's look at a schema and table creation example:

- `token_id (int)`: A unique identifier for each token

- `token (varchar)`: The actual token

- `frequency (int)`: The frequency of the token's occurrence in the dataset (optional but useful for analysis)

- `document_id (int)`: A reference ID linking the token to the original document or source it came from:

```
CREATE TABLE llm_token_data (
    token_id bigint,
    token text,
    frequency bigint,
    document_ids list<bigint>,
    PRIMARY KEY (token_id)
);
```

Distributed filesystems or databases will need to be used to store these very large datasets since they will require distributed storage and processing.

Now that we've ingested and processed the relevant model training data, we can move on to the model pre-training and fine-tuning stage. This stage will provide a usable LLM for a particular application.

Model pre-training and fine-tuning

The processes of pre-training and fine-tuning are fundamental in the life cycle of LLMOps. These steps are pivotal in preparing models, especially transformer-based ones, to understand and generate language effectively.

Pre-training

Let's run through the pre-training process of the sentence *"the recent advancements in AI"* for a transformer model. This sentence is first tokenized `into ["the", "recent", "advance", "ments", "in", ...]` and then applied to the vocabulary mapping we previously created – that is, `{"the": 0, "recent": 1, "advance": 2, "ments": 3, "in": 4, ...}`. Each token gets converted into its corresponding ID based on the vocabulary mapping:

```
["the", "recent", "advance", "ments", "in", ...] [0, 1, 2, 3, 4, ...]
```

In models similar to Llama 2, which typically follow an autoregressive approach to language modeling, the training process involves predicting the next token in a sequence based on the preceding tokens. For example, given the tokens `[0, 1, 2]`, the model aims to predict `"ments"` (ID `'3'`) as the next token. This training process encourages the model to learn the probabilities of token sequences, thereby developing a statistical distribution of language structure and context.

The model's predictions are compared against the actual IDs, and a loss is calculated. This loss quantifies the model's error in prediction. If the model incorrectly predicts 5 instead of 2 for `"advance"`, the loss function captures this error. The model uses this feedback to adjust its internal parameters, improving its predictive accuracy over time.

Fine-tuning

In this scenario, we aim to fine-tune the Llama 2 model, originally trained with a broad understanding of language, so that it specializes in **question-and-answer (Q&A)** tasks related to news articles. This specialization involves honing the model's capabilities in understanding journalistic content and reasoning accurately to respond to queries based on news articles.

For this purpose, we'll isolate a dataset comprising news articles, editorials, and journalistic pieces along with questions about them.

For example, assume we have the sentence *"Economic growth in the last quarter showed a steady increase due to rising tech industry investments."* In this case, the associated Q&A fine-tuning pair that we could use would be as follows:

- Question: *"What contributed to the economic growth in the last quarter?"*

- Answer: *"Rising tech industry investments."*

This pair would be combined into a single sequence: *"What contributed to the economic growth in the last quarter? Economic growth in the last quarter showed a steady increase due to rising tech industry investments."*

This sentence would be tokenized:

```
["What", "contributed", "to", "the", "economic", "growth", "in",
 "the", "last", "quarter", "?", "Economic", "growth", "in", "the",
 "last", "quarter", "showed", "a", "steady", "increase", "due", "to",
 "rising", "tech", "industry", "investments", "."]
```

After tokenizing the sentence, the tokens are then mapped to a vocabulary of unique IDs: `[7, 8, 1, 5 ...]`.

These unique ID mappings are used by the model instead of actual text to allow for more efficient calculations instead of performing mathematical operations on text-based strings. In pretraining, these mappings are used to predict the subsequent tokens given an original token sequence. The loss calculations are applied to ensure the LLM parameters are optimized further for the news Q&A use case.

Sliding windows

In the fine-tuning process of a language model such as Llama 2, the sliding window technique is utilized to manage sequences that exceed the model's maximum token processing capacity. This technique is essential for ensuring that each part of a long sequence contributes to the model's training, particularly when dealing with extensive textual data.

Implementation of the sliding window technique

The process begins by setting the parameters for the sliding window. In our scenario, the window size is set to accommodate a maximum of 10 tokens at any given time. Additionally, we establish a shift size of 5 tokens, which determines the step size for moving the window across the sequence.

For the given sequence, we have `["What"`, `"contributed"`, `"to"`, `"the"`, `"economic"`, `"growth"`, `"in"`, `"the"`, `"last"`, `"quarter"`, `"?"`, `"Economic"`, `"growth"`, `"in"`, `"the"`, `"last"`, `"quarter"`, `"showed"`, `"a"`, `"steady"`, `"increase"`, `"due"`, `"to"`, `"rising"`, `"tech"`, `"industry"`, `"investments"`, `"."]` - the first window encapsulates the initial 10 tokens: `["What"`, `"contributed"`, `"to"`, `"the"`, `"economic"`, `"growth"`, `"in"`, `"the"`, `"last"`, `"quarter"]`. This window provides a contextual snippet for the model to learn from.

After processing the first window, the window shifts forward by the predetermined 5 tokens. This shift repositions the starting token of the next window to `"growth,"` changing the focus of the text being processed and ensuring that different parts of the sequence are learned.

The process continues with the second window covering the tokens from `"growth,"` to `"showed,"` and so on. Each shift moves the window 5 tokens ahead, allowing the model to sequentially process overlapping segments of the sequence. This overlap is crucial as it ensures continuity in learning, providing the model with a more cohesive understanding of the text.

The final window in this sequence might differ in size, depending on the remaining tokens. In cases where fewer than 10 tokens are left, the window simply adjusts to include all remaining tokens, such as `["to"`, `"rising"`, `"tech"`, `"industry"`, `"investments"`, `"."]`. This ensures that even the tail end of the sequence contributes to the model's training.

Sliding window nuances

The selection of sliding window sizes is a nuanced decision that's influenced by factors such as the model's architectural limits, the nature of the task at hand, and available computational resources. For instance, in models such as BERT, which has a maximum token capacity of 512, the window size for fine-tuning is often dictated by this limit. However, practical applications usually opt for smaller sizes for efficiency, commonly ranging from 128 to 256 tokens for tasks requiring detailed linguistic analysis. These sizes are sufficient for providing a deep contextual understanding without overwhelming computational resources.

In contrast, for tasks necessitating a broader context, such as document summarization or complex question answering that spans larger text segments, window sizes might approach the upper limit, such as 384 or even the full 512 tokens. This larger window allows the model to encompass a more extensive context, which is crucial for understanding and generating coherent responses or summaries in such tasks.

The shift size, or the stride with which the window moves across the text, is another critical factor. Typically, this is set to a fraction of the window size, often between 50% and 75%, ensuring a significant overlap in the text segments being analyzed. For example, a window size of 256 tokens might be paired with a shift size of around 128 to 192 tokens, providing continuity in the model's exposure to the text.

The choice of window size also balances the need for context against computational efficiency. Larger windows, while contextually rich, demand more computational power and can prolong training times. Therefore, a strategic balance is often sought, especially in fine-tuning, which is more task-specific than pre-training. For instance, in fine-tuning a model for sentence-level tasks, smaller windows that encapsulate one or two sentences might be preferred, whereas paragraph-level analysis might warrant larger windows that can include several sentences or an entire paragraph.

Task-specific requirements also play a significant role in determining the window size. For example, in a task that revolves around understanding the relationship between consecutive sentences or paragraphs, larger window sizes that can cover multiple sentences or a whole paragraph would be more effective.

Now that we have a trained LLM, we can move on to model governance and review. These items are important factors in determining whether a model can be deployed to a production environment.

Governance and review

Governance and review are crucial aspects of managing LLMs in LLMOps, ensuring that the models are secure, compliant with regulations, and functionally robust. This process involves safeguarding against data leakage, controlling access to information, thorough evaluation of model performance, and adherence to legal standards such as the **General Data Protection Regulation (GDPR)**.

Avoiding training data leakage

When developing and training LLMs, we need to prevent what is known as **training data leakage**. This term refers to the inadvertent incorporation of sensitive information from the training dataset into the model's knowledge base, potentially leading to significant privacy breaches. Such breaches not only compromise individual privacy but can also have broader implications for data protection and trust in AI systems.

To combat this, one effective strategy that's employed is **data anonymization**. Before the training data is fed into the model, any sensitive information, especially personal identifiers or traceable data, is carefully anonymized or completely removed. This process involves altering or encrypting personal identifiers so that the individuals to whom the data pertains cannot be easily identified, thereby safeguarding their privacy:

```
["Patient", "John", "Doe", "born", "on", "July", "7", "1980", "has",
"been", "diagnosed", "with", "diabetes"]
->
["Patient", "[Name]", "born", "on", "[Date]", "has", "been",
"diagnosed", "with", "diabetes"]
```

Another approach is to implement **differential privacy techniques** during the model training phase. Differential privacy is a system for publicly sharing information about a dataset by describing patterns of groups within the dataset while withholding information about individuals in the dataset. For instance, consider the previous example:

```
["Patient", "John", "Doe", "born", "on", "July", "7", "1980", "has",
"been", "diagnosed", "with", "diabetes"]
```

When applying differential privacy, this age and name might be randomly adjusted. The modification is minor and does not substantially alter the statistical properties of the dataset, but it effectively prevents the model from learning and later reproducing exact details from individual patient records:

```
["Patient", "SubjectA", "born", "on", "June", "30", "1980", "has",
"been", "diagnosed", "with", "diabetes"]
```

Subsequently, the LLM is trained on this modified, "noised" version of the dataset. The outcome of this training process is a model that has learned the general patterns, such as common treatments for certain age groups or symptoms, without being able to identify or reveal precise details from specific patient records.

Access control

In this section, we'll cover controlling access to the knowledge contained within an LLM. The goal is to ensure that different users or user groups only access information that is relevant and permissible for their specific roles. To achieve this, a systematic approach involving user segmentation, **role-based access control (RBAC)**, and careful data management is essential.

At the core of this approach is the implementation of RBAC, where users are categorized into distinct roles such as administrator, developer, analyst, and end user, each with tailored access privileges. These roles define the scope of actions a user can perform and the extent of the model's knowledge they can access.

Complementing this system is the development of different interfaces or APIs for interacting with the LLM. Each interface is designed to cater to specific user roles, limiting the functionality to what's necessary and appropriate for each role. For example, an interface for an end user may restrict access to only basic queries, whereas a developer's interface might offer broader functionalities, including insights into the model's training data:

```
Administrator:
    - /modelManagement
    - /userAccessControl
    - /systemSettings
Developer:
    - /modelDetails
    - /trainingDataInsights
```

```
      - /debuggingTools
Analyst:
   - /queryModel
   - /resultAnalysis
End-User:
   - /simpleQuery
   - /help
```

Additionally, safeguarding the model's knowledge involves query and output filtering mechanisms. These filters scrutinize user queries and outputs, ensuring they align with the user's access permissions. The aim is to prevent users from retrieving information outside their authorized scope. Data partitioning also plays a vital role. Here, the training data is segmented and different model instances are trained on these segments. Users are then provided access to the model version that aligns with their role-specific data segment:

```
# End-User Interaction
> ROLE: End-User
> QUERY: "What was the amount of my last deposit?"
# System checks role and query validity
> RESPONSE: "Your last deposit was $500."

In this above case, access is granted since the query pertains to the
user's own account information. Let's see another example.
# End-User Attempting Unauthorized Access
> ROLE: End-User
> QUERY: "Show me the transaction history for account number 987654."
# System recognizes role and evaluates query scope
> RESPONSE: "Access to the requested information is restricted."
```

In this case, access is denied since the query pertains to another user's account information. Let's look at another example:

```
# Analyst Interaction
> ROLE: Analyst
> QUERY: "Provide the latest report on mortgage rate trends."
# System identifies role and validates query context
> RESPONSE: "Latest mortgage rate trends report: [Report Details]."
```

In this case, access is granted since the query pertains to approved information. Let's see another example:

```
# Analyst Attempting Unauthorized Access
> ROLE: Analyst
> QUERY: "Give me the account details for John Doe."
# System checks role and query authorization
```

```
> RESPONSE: "You do not have access to individual customer account
details."
  In this case, access is denied since the analyst's query pertains to
an individual customer. Let's see another example.


# Administrator Interaction
> ROLE: Administrator
> QUERY: "Update the risk assessment model parameters."
# System verifies administrator privileges
> RESPONSE: "Risk assessment model parameters updated successfully."
  In this case, access is granted since the admin's query pertains to
the model parameters.
```

Regular audits and continuous monitoring of user interactions with the model are crucial. These processes help in identifying any discrepancies or unauthorized access attempts, ensuring the access control mechanisms are functioning as intended. Lastly, underpinning these technical measures are robust legal and policy frameworks. Clear usage policies establish the boundaries of what each user role can and cannot do with the model. Enforcing user agreements as part of the access protocol ensures that all users are aware of and adhere to these policies, thereby maintaining a controlled and secure interaction with the LLM.

Review

Evaluating the performance of an LLM involves a variety of metrics, each designed to assess different aspects of the model's linguistic capabilities and contextual accuracy. The metrics we'll cover include **perplexity**, **human evaluation**, **Bilingual Evaluation Understudy** (**BLEU**), and **diversity**.

Perplexity measures the model's ability to predict a sample. In this context, a lower perplexity score is indicative of better predictive performance, signifying that the model can more accurately anticipate the next word or sequence in each text:

```
Context: The cat sat on the
Prediction: mat
Perplexity Score: 5
```

The model predicts mat following The cat sat on the, which is a logical and common continuation. The low perplexity score of 5 reflects the model's high confidence and accuracy in this prediction. This is a typical example of a predictable and straightforward context for the model:

```
Context: To infinity and
Prediction: apple
Perplexity Score: 150
```

The model's prediction of `apple` for the context `To infinity` and is unexpected and contextually inaccurate. The high perplexity score of `150` indicates the model's uncertainty and error in this prediction. This example highlights a lack of contextual understanding, leading to a high perplexity score.

Another crucial component of evaluation is **human evaluation**, which brings a subjective but essential perspective to the model's assessment. Here, human reviewers critically analyze the outputs generated by the LLM, focusing on their relevance, coherence, and overall accuracy. This method helps to gauge how well the model's responses align with human expectations and linguistic standards.

For models specialized in translation, the **BLEU** metric is commonly used. BLEU is a quantitative measure of how closely the model's translated output matches a set of high-quality reference translations. It's a key indicator of the model's effectiveness in capturing the nuances of different languages and accurately conveying the intended meaning.

Lastly, **diversity** is another important metric, especially for models that are used in creative or varied contexts. This metric evaluates the range and variety of the model's outputs. A model scoring high in diversity can generate multiple, distinct responses or solutions to a given prompt, showcasing its flexibility and creativity. This is particularly valuable in applications where varied responses are desirable, such as in conversational AI or content generation:

```
Context: "What is the weather like in"
Predictions:
1. New York
2. Paris
3. Tokyo
4. Sydney
5. Toronto
Diversity Score: High
```

Given the context `What is the weather like in`, the model generates diverse predictions: `New York`, `Paris`, `Tokyo`, `Sydney`, and `Toronto`. This range of predictions across different global cities reflects a high diversity score. The model demonstrates its ability to produce varied and contextually relevant responses, indicating it has a robust understanding of the open-ended nature of the query:

```
Context: "Best ways to cook"
Predictions:
1. Pasta
2. Pasta
3. Pasta
4. Pasta
5. Pasta
Diversity Score: Low
```

For the context `Best ways to cook`, the model repetitively predicts `Pasta`. The lack of variation in the predictions leads to a low diversity score. This example shows the model's limited ability to generate varied responses, suggesting a need for improvement in its response generation diversity.

Together, these metrics provide a comprehensive picture of an LLM's performance, offering insights into its strengths and areas for improvement. By employing a combination of quantitative measures such as perplexity and BLEU, along with qualitative assessments through human evaluation and diversity checks, developers and researchers can ensure that the LLMs they are working with are robust, accurate, and effectively aligned with their intended applications.

Regulatory compliance

Ensuring compliance with regulations such as GDPR is a critical aspect of managing LLMOps, especially concerning user data privacy and provisioning the right to explanation. To align with GDPR requirements, several implementation strategies are essential.

Firstly, data processing transparency is paramount. LLMS must maintain clarity in how they process and utilize user data. This involves openly communicating to users how their data is being used by the model, ensuring that there are no hidden processes or ambiguous uses of personal information. Transparency helps build user trust and aligns with the GDPR's emphasis on clear and lawful processing of personal data.

Additionally, the right to erasure and data portability are fundamental components of GDPR compliance. Users must have the ability to request the deletion of their data, often referred to as the **right to be forgotten**. Moreover, they should be able to request the portability of their data, which means they can obtain and reuse their data for their own purposes across different services. Implementing these rights requires LLMs to have mechanisms in place that allow users to easily make such requests and for these requests to be acted upon efficiently.

Regular audits are also a critical part of ensuring ongoing compliance. These audits involve reviewing and assessing the LLM's data processing practices, ensuring they consistently meet GDPR standards. Regular audits help in identifying and rectifying any compliance issues, thus maintaining the LLM's alignment with GDPR requirements over time.

Now that we've confirmed that the LLM has passed the review and governance stages, we can move on to inference, serving, and scalability. This stage ensures the LLM can produce predictions in production reliably.

Inference, serving, and scalability

In the realm of LLMs, the topics of inference, serving, and scalability are crucial for efficient operation and optimal user experience. These aspects cover how the model's insights are delivered (**inference**), how they are served to the end users (**serving**), and how the system adapts to varying loads (**scalability**).

Online and batch inference

Inference can be mainly categorized into online and batch processing. **Online inference** refers to the real-time processing of individual queries, where responses are generated instantly. On the other hand, **batch inference** deals with processing large volumes of queries at once, which is more efficient for tasks that don't require immediate responses.

For instance, for a conversational AI chatbot used by a large retail company, online inference plays a crucial role. The chatbot is tasked with interacting with customers in real time, answering their queries, resolving issues, and providing product information. The nature of this interaction requires immediate response to each unique query to maintain a smooth, conversational flow. When a customer asks a question such as *"What are the shipping options for my location?"*, the chatbot relies on online inference to instantly process this input and generate a relevant response. This immediate processing capability is key to ensuring that the chatbot can engage effectively with customers, thus enhancing the overall user experience and the efficiency of customer service.

On the other hand, batch inference is more suited to sentiment analysis performed on customer reviews for a new product launched by a tech company. In this case, the goal is to aggregate and analyze extensive sets of customer reviews to gauge overall sentiment and identify common themes or issues. Reviews collected over a certain period, such as a week, are processed in a single batch. This approach allows for a comprehensive analysis of the data, providing insights into customer opinions and trends over that period. Here, the efficiency lies in processing large datasets simultaneously, as opposed to the real-time response required in the chatbot scenario.

CPU versus GPU serving

When it comes to serving these inferences, the choice between using **central processing units** (**CPUs**) and **graphics processing units** (**GPUs**) can significantly impact performance.

CPUs are known for their versatility and cost-effectiveness. They are generally sufficient for handling smaller or less complex models where the demand for parallel processing isn't as intense. CPUs are particularly advantageous in applications where low latency is crucial and the computational load is moderate, making them suitable for efficient performance in such scenarios. From a budgetary standpoint, CPUs are often more economical due to their lower upfront and operational costs compared to GPUs. This makes them a preferred choice in scenarios where budget constraints are significant. Additionally, their suitability for general-purpose computing tasks, which require a wide range of computing capabilities beyond just machine learning, adds to their versatility.

GPUs, however, are more adept at handling large and complex LLMs, such as GPT-3 or BERT. These models often need to process large sequences of data in parallel, a task for which GPUs are particularly well-suited. In high-throughput scenarios, where the system needs to manage a high volume of simultaneous inference requests, GPUs can significantly enhance throughput, thereby offering a performance advantage. Although GPUs have higher energy demands, their ability to handle more computations per unit of energy makes them more efficient for operations at a larger scale. This efficiency is particularly evident when models leverage advanced neural network features that benefit from parallel processing, such as multiple layers of transformers.

In some cases, a hybrid approach that utilizes both CPUs and GPUs can be effective. This strategy involves handling routine tasks with CPUs, while more computationally intensive tasks are delegated to GPUs. Such an approach allows for a balance between cost and performance efficiency. Modern serving frameworks often employ dynamic allocation, which can intelligently assign tasks to CPUs or GPUs based on the current load and the complexity of the computations required. This ensures optimal utilization of resources.

When considering scalability, it's essential to assess how easily each option can be scaled to meet changing demands. This is especially important for services that need to rapidly scale up or down.

Containerized deployments

When deploying LLMs using containerization, the model, along with all its dependencies, libraries, and a specific runtime environment, is packaged into a container. This packaging approach facilitates seamless and consistent deployments across various computing environments. Containerization tools such as Docker are prevalently used for this purpose. They create container images that encapsulate everything the model requires to function, ensuring that the model runs the same way, irrespective of where the container is deployed.

However, for containers to effectively leverage the processing power of GPUs, specialized configurations are necessary. This involves using GPU-enabled base images in the container and installing the appropriate drivers and libraries, such as **CUDA** and **cuDNN**, which are essential for GPU acceleration and compatibility. These configurations ensure that the container can access and utilize GPU resources, which is critical for the performance-intensive computations typical of LLMs.

Deploying GPUs in containerized environments for LLMs brings with it a series of potential challenges that need careful consideration, including combability, resource allocation, orchestration, monitoring, debugging, and security.

Now that the LLM has been deployed to production, we'll need to monitor it to ensure that there's no variation from expected performance over time.

Monitoring

Monitoring and continuous improvement are vital components in the management of LLMs and encompass a wide range of metrics and processes. Key performance indicators, such as the number of requests, response time, token usage, costs, and error rates, are crucial for assessing the efficiency and effectiveness of these models. Tracking the number of requests helps in understanding the load and demand on the system, while response time is indicative of the model's speed and user experience. Monitoring token usage is essential, especially when token-based pricing strategies are in place, as it directly impacts the cost-effectiveness of the model's operation. Additionally, keeping a close eye on error rates is imperative to ensure the accuracy and reliability of the LLM's outputs. Collectively, these metrics provide a comprehensive view of the LLM's performance, enabling administrators to make informed decisions for resource allocation, scaling, and cost management:

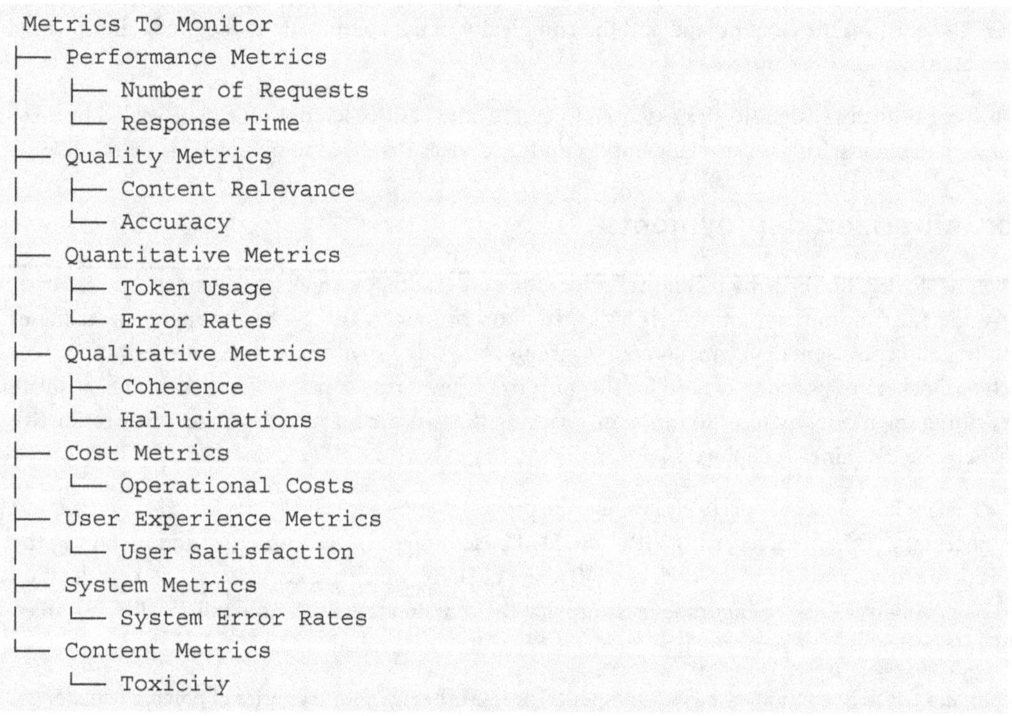

```
Metrics To Monitor
├── Performance Metrics
│   ├── Number of Requests
│   └── Response Time
├── Quality Metrics
│   ├── Content Relevance
│   └── Accuracy
├── Quantitative Metrics
│   ├── Token Usage
│   └── Error Rates
├── Qualitative Metrics
│   ├── Coherence
│   └── Hallucinations
├── Cost Metrics
│   └── Operational Costs
├── User Experience Metrics
│   └── User Satisfaction
├── System Metrics
│   └── System Error Rates
└── Content Metrics
    └── Toxicity
```

Further refinement in monitoring involves the use of **evaluator LLMs**, which are specifically designed to assess the quality of outputs from the primary LLM. These evaluators play a critical role in ensuring the outputs meet the desired standards of relevance, accuracy, and coherence. Alongside this, output monitoring for toxicity, relevance, and hallucinations is crucial for maintaining the integrity and usefulness of the model. Monitoring toxicity is particularly important to prevent the generation of harmful or offensive content. Relevance monitoring ensures that the LLM's responses or outputs are aligned with the input prompts, providing meaningful and contextually appropriate information. Additionally, keeping an eye out for hallucinations – instances where the model generates factually incorrect or nonsensical information – is critical to maintaining the trustworthiness and reliability of the LLM. These monitoring processes not only aid in maintaining the quality of the model but also serve as a foundation for continuous improvement, feeding into the model's ongoing training and development to enhance its performance over time.

Continuous improvement

In the realm of LLMs such as GPT, continuous improvement is paramount to maintaining their relevance and efficacy. This process is multifaceted and involves integrating new data, developing strategies to prevent previous knowledge from being forgotten, and incorporating human feedback.

Firstly, incorporating newer data is essential as language and societal contexts evolve. Regular updates with recent datasets ensure that models grasp current terminologies, phrases, and relevant topics. This could involve data from diverse sources, such as the latest news articles, scientific publications, and trending internet content. Such updates help the model stay current with linguistic trends and societal changes.

Secondly, a significant challenge in training neural networks, especially when they learn new information, is avoiding catastrophic forgetting. This phenomenon occurs when a model loses the information it had learned previously upon acquiring new knowledge. Techniques such as **elastic weight consolidation** (**EWC**) and progressive neural networks are employed to mitigate this. These methods prioritize the balance between retaining learned knowledge and adapting to new data, thus maintaining the model's overall performance across a broad spectrum of topics.

Lastly, human feedback plays a crucial role in refining LLM outputs. This feedback helps ensure that the model's responses are not only accurate but also contextually and emotionally congruent with human expectations. Methods such as **reinforcement learning from human feedback** (**RLHF**) involve training models on a mix of existing data and inputs from human evaluators who assess the quality and relevance of the model's responses. This process is vital for aligning the model's output with ethical standards and societal values, thereby enhancing reliability and user trust.

Incorporating human feedback is particularly important as it provides a necessary check against the model's learning biases and errors, ensuring that outputs are both technically sound and socially appropriate. As language models continue to evolve, these strategies ensure they remain effective tools capable of understanding and generating human language in a manner that is both useful and responsible.

Summary

This chapter provided a review of each component in the LLMOps landscape by iterating through data preparation, model development, governance and review, model serving, and monitoring. In the next chapter, we'll dive deeper into data preparation.

Part 2:

Tools and Strategies in LLMOps

Part two covers the practical aspects of implementing LLMOps, focusing on the critical stages of data management, including collection, transformation, and preparation, which are essential for training effective LLMs. Then, we explore the steps involved in model development, from feature creation to hyperparameter tuning. Finally, we address the crucial aspects of evaluating model performance, securing models, and ensuring they comply with legal and regulatory standards. This section provides a comprehensive look at the operational processes that ensure LLMs are both effective and adhere to required norms and practices.

This part contains the following chapters:

- *Chapter 3, Processing Data in LLMOps Tools*
- *Chapter 4, Developing Models via LLMOps*
- *Chapter 5, LLMOps Review and Compliance*

3

Processing Data in LLMOps Tools

Data preparation for textual data, whether it's structured, semi-structured, or unstructured, involves a series of steps designed to understand the dataset's characteristics, identify patterns, and prepare the data for further analysis or modeling. In the context of **large language models (LLMs)**, this step is crucial in ensuring the data's quality and relevance before training with it. This chapter outlines an end-to-end workflow for preparing textual data and explores the following topics:

- Collecting data

- Transforming data

- Preparing data

- Automating data

Collecting data

Data collection is a critical first step in preparing a dataset for training LLMs. Let's go through an example of preparing a dataset for an LLM-based Chrome extension that provides a **Question & Answer (Q&A)** interface for webpages that a user navigates to. This process involves gathering data from various sources, each of which can present unique challenges and opportunities for model training. Let's review a few types of textual data that we're likely to encounter.

Collecting structured data

Structured data is highly organized and easily readable by machines. It is typically stored in databases, spreadsheets, or CSV files. Each record adheres to a fixed schema with clearly defined columns and data types, making it straightforward to process and analyze. For instance, a file containing a list of **Frequently Asked Questions (FAQs)** and their answers from a company's website can be used in training. Let's go through that process here.

Imagine that we have a Parquet file (`faqs.snappy.parquet`) containing a list of FAQs and their answers, sourced from a company's website. The structure of the data in this Parquet file could resemble the following pandas DataFrame table:

```
+-------------------------------+-------------------------------+
| question                      | answer                        |
+-------------------------------+-------------------------------+
| How can I reset my pa...      | You can reset your passwo...|
+-------------------------------+-------------------------------+
| What is the return po...      | Our return policy is 30...    |
+-------------------------------+-------------------------------+
| How should I track my...      | You can track your orders...|
+-------------------------------+-------------------------------+
```

We'll need to do the following to collect the data:

1. **Load Parquet file**: Use pandas and s3fs to read the Parquet file from the specified S3 bucket path.

2. **Convert to a list**: Extract the question and answer columns from the DataFrame and convert them into lists.

3. **Create a new DataFrame**: Form a new DataFrame from the list of questions and answers.

4. **Convert to CSV and upload**: The new DataFrame is converted into the CSV format using StringIO and then uploaded back to S3 as a CSV file.

This process effectively transforms structured data from a Parquet format to a CSV format, making it more accessible or suitable for different applications or further processing needs. This example demonstrates a typical workflow for handling structured data within a cloud environment, leveraging popular Python libraries for data manipulation and AWS services for storage. Here's the full code snippet to collect the structured data:

```python
import pandas as pd
import s3fs
import boto3
from io import StringIO


s3_bucket_path = 's3://your-bucket-name/path-to-your-file/faqs.snappy.parquet'


fs = s3fs.S3FileSystem()


df = pd.read_parquet(s3_bucket_path, engine='pyarrow', filesystem=fs)


questions = df['question'].tolist()
```

```
answers = df['answer'].tolist()

df_new = pd.DataFrame({'question': questions, 'answer': answers})

csv_buffer = StringIO()
df_new.to_csv(csv_buffer, index=False)

csv_buffer.seek(0)

s3_resource = boto3.resource('s3')
bucket_name = 'your-bucket-name'  # Replace with your actual bucket
name
object_key = 'path/to/your-new-file/questions_answers.csv'

s3_resource.Object(bucket_name,
    object_key).put(Body=csv_buffer.getvalue())
```

Now that we have collected the structured data into a CSV file, let's move on to semi-structured data.

Collecting semi-structured data

Semi-structured data doesn't have a rigid structure like structured data, but it does have organizational properties that make it easier to analyze than unstructured data. JSON and XML are common formats, offering flexibility in data representation and a hierarchical structure for nesting information. As an example, JSON files exported from a customer service platform such as Jira, containing inquiry tickets with questions categorized by issue type, response texts, and metadata, can be used to help train our model. Let's run through an example that assumes the Jira API returns the following elements:

- `ticket_id`: A unique identifier for each ticket

- `issue_type`: Categorization of the ticket's subject matter

- `question`: The user's inquiry or problem statement

- `response`: The provided solution or answer to the user's question

- `metadata`: The created and updated dates and tags

- `created_at`: The timestamp when the ticket was created

- `updated_at`: The timestamp when the ticket was last updated

- `tags`: Keywords associated with the ticket for categorization or searchability

Let's also assume that the results are returned in JSON format:

```
{
  "tickets": [
    {
      "ticket_id": "TICKET123",
      "issue_type": "Account Access",
      "question": "How can I recover my account?",
      "response": "To recover your account, please use the 'Forgot
Password' option on the login page or contact support for further
assistance.",
      "metadata": {
        "created_at": "2023-01-15T09:30:00Z",
        "updated_at": "2023-01-16T10:00:00Z",
        "tags": ["account", "recovery", "support"]
      }
    },
    {
      "ticket_id": "TICKET456",
      "issue_type": "Payment Issue",
      "question": "Why was my payment declined?",
      "response": "Payments can be declined for several reasons,
including insufficient funds, incorrect card details, or bank
restrictions. Please review your payment method or contact your bank
for more information.",
      "metadata": {
        "created_at": "2023-01-20T11:20:00Z",
        "updated_at": "2023-01-20T12:35:00Z",
        "tags": ["payment", "declined", "billing"]
      }
    },
  ]
}
```

Let's now write this code process that fetches the data elements from Jira and transforms it into a Q&A
CSV to be uploaded into an S3 bucket out end-to-end:

```python
import requests
import pandas as pd
import boto3
from io import StringIO


API_URL = "https://example.com/api/tickets"
S3_BUCKET = "your-bucket-name"
S3_KEY = "path/to/your-file/questions_answers.csv"
```

```python
AWS_ACCESS_KEY_ID = 'your-access-key'
AWS_SECRET_ACCESS_KEY = 'your-secret-key'

def save_to_s3(df, bucket, key):
    csv_buffer = StringIO()
    df.to_csv(csv_buffer, index=False)
    s3_client = boto3.client('s3',
        aws_access_key_id=AWS_ACCESS_KEY_ID,
        aws_secret_access_key=AWS_SECRET_ACCESS_KEY)
    s3_client.put_object(Bucket=bucket, Key=key,
        Body=csv_buffer.getvalue())
    print(f"Successfully uploaded {key} to {bucket}")
```

The preceding code imports required packages, defines constants, and adds a function that saves data to S3. This will allow us to get into the processing flow that follows:

```python
def fetch_data(api_url):
    response = requests.get(api_url)
    if response.status_code == 200:
        return response.json()
    else:
        print("Failed to fetch data")
        return None

def process_data(json_data):
    tickets = json_data.get("tickets", [])
    data = [{"question": ticket["question"],
        "answer": ticket["response"]} for ticket in tickets]
    return pd.DataFrame(data)

json_data = fetch_data(API_URL)
if json_data:
    df = process_data(json_data)
    save_to_s3(df, S3_BUCKET, S3_KEY)
```

This code defines three functions that cumulatively assist in processing the data, including fetching semi-structured data from an API and extracting it into a CSV format. Now that we've shown how to collect semi-structured data, let's look at collecting unstructured data.

Collecting unstructured data

Unstructured data is not organized in a predefined manner, making it the most challenging to process and analyze. This category includes text files, documents, emails, and web pages, where the information is presented as free-form text. We'll want to incorporate web pages and their FAQs in our data to properly train the LLM to be able to answer questions about a webpage. Here's an example of what the unstructured data, a webpage, looks like:

```html
<!DOCTYPE html>
<html lang="en">
<head>
    <meta charset="UTF-8">
    <title>FAQ Page</title>
</head>
<body>
    <div class="faq-section">
        <h2>How can I reset my password?</h2>
        <p>You can reset your password by going to the settings page
and selecting the 'Reset Password' option.</p>

        <h2>What is the return policy?</h2>
        <p>Our return policy lasts 30 days. If 30 days have gone by
since your purchase, unfortunately, we can't offer you a refund or
exchange.</p>

        <h2>How do I track my order?</h2>
        <p>Once your order has been shipped, you will receive a
tracking number that allows you to follow your package's journey to
your doorstep.</p>
    </div>
</body>
</html>
```

Let's look at a code snippet that can process this unstructured text, HTML, into a CSV file for easier data analysis and model fine-tuning:

```python
import requests
from bs4 import BeautifulSoup
import pandas as pd
import boto3
from io import StringIO


def save_df_to_s3(
    df, bucket_name, object_name, aws_access_key_id,
    aws_secret_access_key
```

```python
):
    csv_buffer = StringIO()
    df.to_csv(csv_buffer, index=False)
    s3_resource = boto3.resource('s3',
        aws_access_key_id=aws_access_key_id,
        aws_secret_access_key=aws_secret_access_key)
    s3_resource.Object(
        bucket_name,
        object_name
    ).put(Body=csv_buffer.getvalue())
    print(f"File {object_name} saved to bucket {bucket_name}.")
```

The preceding code imports the required libraries and implements a function that saves a DataFrame to S3. Let's look at the rest of the code now:

```python
def fetch_faq_page(url):
    response = requests.get(url)
    if response.status_code == 200:
        soup = BeautifulSoup(response.text, 'html.parser')
        faq_sections = soup.find_all(class_='faq-section')
        faqs = []
        for section in faq_sections:
            questions = section.find_all('h2')  # Assuming questions
are wrapped in <h2> tags
            answers = [q.find_next_sibling('p') for q in questions]
            faqs += [{'question': q.text.strip(),
                'answer': a.text.strip()
                } for q, a in zip(questions, answers) if a]
        return faqs
    else:
        print("Failed to fetch the page.")
        return []
```

The preceding function implements a way to scrape a website. It extracts the scraped data into a structured format. Let's now look at the main function of the code:

```python
def main():
    FAQ_URL = "https://example.com/faqs"
    AWS_ACCESS_KEY_ID = 'your_access_key'
    AWS_SECRET_ACCESS_KEY = 'your_secret_key'
    S3_BUCKET = 'your_bucket_name'
    S3_OBJECT_NAME = 'faqs.csv'

    faq_data = fetch_faq_page(FAQ_URL)
```

```
if faq_data:
    df_faqs = pd.DataFrame(faq_data)
    save_df_to_s3(df_faqs, S3_BUCKET, S3_OBJECT_NAME,
        AWS_ACCESS_KEY_ID, AWS_SECRET_ACCESS_KEY)
else:
    print("No data fetched or saved.")
```

The preceding code allows us to scrape FAQs from a website, assuming that the site's `robot.txt` file allows it, and transforms it into a CSV and uploads it to S3.

Now, let's get this collected CSV data into a single, unified dataset to facilitate data exploration and model training.

Transforming data

Transforming the data into a centralized repository is a critical step in preparing for effective data analysis and model training, particularly with LLMs. Let's go through the detailed process of organizing, cleaning, and processing data from various sources—structured, semi-structured, and unstructured—into a cohesive repository. Each data type presents unique challenges and requires tailored approaches to ensure its utility in enhancing model performance. We will explore the strategies and methodologies necessary to construct such a repository, laying the groundwork for the data to be readily accessible and in an optimal state for both analysis and the training of sophisticated LLMs.

Defining core data attributes

The data structure definition, referred to as a schema, must encapsulate core attributes that are common across all data types, ensuring they are tailored for a Q&A context. This involves the inclusion of the following:

- `QuestionID`: A unique identifier for each Q&A instance facilitates easy reference and management of data

- `Question`: The text of the question itself

- `Answer`: The text that provides the answer to the corresponding question

- `DataSource`: Identifies the origin of the data, such as CSV for structured data, Jira for semi-structured data, or Website for unstructured data

- `Provenance`: Captures the origin details of the data, including URLs for web content, filenames for JSON exports, or descriptors for other sources

- `Context`: Includes chunked text from web pages that provide background or additional information relevant to the Q&A pair

You'll notice that we didn't cover `Context` when collecting Q&A data from various sources. This is because human labelers will be required to produce and associate relevant contexts in the training examples. In the following fine-tuning example, the context is relevant to both the question and the appropriate answer. It also provides a foundation to create a consistent Q&A training example:

```
Context: If you've forgotten your password or wish to change it for
security reasons, resetting your password is simple. Follow our step-
by-step guide on the password reset page.
Question: How can I reset my password?
Answer: To reset your password, navigate to the settings page, select
'Password Reset,' and follow the instructions.
```

We'll later show how to automatically generate the `Context` for the Q&A LLM application. Assuming that we have contexts for a fine-tuning example, here's a Python dictionary representing a complete data entry based on the preceding schema:

```python
transformed_data_example = {
    "QuestionID": "Q123456789",
    "Question": "What is the return policy?",
    "Answer": "Our return policy lasts 30 days...",
    "DataSource": "CSV",
    "Provenance": "faq_list.csv",
    "Context": "Returns and Exchanges are honored..."
}
```

The preceding example showcases the desired structure of the data after its transformation, including its metadata. Let's look at how to implement this.

Transforming data

The data that we collected at the beginning of the chapter has already been transformed into the CSV format with questions and answers as columns. Let's review a Python script that can conduct a transformation for these columns to produce a unified data repository that matches the preceding data definition:

```python
import pandas as pd
import boto3
import s3fs
from io import BytesIO


AWS_ACCESS_KEY_ID = 'your_access_key'
AWS_SECRET_ACCESS_KEY = 'your_secret_key'
S3_BUCKET = 'your_bucket_name'
```

```python
structured_csv_path = 's3://your_bucket_name/path_to_your_csv/
structured_faq_list.csv'
semi_structured_csv_path = 's3://your_bucket_name/path_to_your_csv/
semi_structured_faq_list.csv'
unstructured_csv_path = 's3://your_bucket_name/path_to_your_csv/
unstructured_faq_list.csv'

output_parquet_path = 's3://your_bucket_name/path_to_output/faq_list.
snappy.parquet'
```

The preceding code imports the required libraries and also defines the needed constants. Next, we'll define the functions to read and write data to S3:

```python
def read_csv_from_s3(s3_path):
    return pd.read_csv(s3_path)


def save_to_s3_as_parquet(
    df, bucket_name, object_name, access_key_id,
    secret_access_key
):
    s3_resource = boto3.resource('s3',
                                 aws_access_key_id=access_key_id,
                                 aws_secret_access_key=secret_access_
key)
    parquet_buffer = BytesIO()
    df.to_parquet(parquet_buffer, index=False, compression='snappy')
    s3_resource.Object(bucket_name,
        object_name).put(Body=parquet_buffer.getvalue())
```

Now that we've defined our `read` and `write` functions, let's transform the data:

```python
def transform_data(df, data_source, provenance):
    df['QuestionID'] = df.index + 1
    df['QuestionID'] = df['QuestionID'].apply(lambda x: f"Q{x:09d}")
    df['DataSource'] = data_source
    df['Provenance'] = provenance.split('/')[-1]
    df['Context'] = "Provide context here manually"
    df = df[['QuestionID', 'Question', 'Answer', 'DataSource',
        'Provenance', 'Context']]

    return df


def process_and_save_data():
    structured_df = read_csv_from_s3(structured_csv_path)
```

```python
semi_structured_df = read_csv_from_s3(semi_structured_csv_path)
unstructured_df = read_csv_from_s3(unstructured_csv_path)

structured_transformed = transform_data(structured_df,
    "CSV", structured_csv_path)
semi_structured_transformed = transform_data(
    semi_structured_df, "Jira", semi_structured_csv_path)
unstructured_transformed = transform_data(
    unstructured_df, "Website", unstructured_csv_path)

final_df = pd.concat(
    [structured_transformed, semi_structured_transformed,
    unstructured_transformed], ignore_index=True)

save_to_s3_as_parquet(final_df, S3_BUCKET,
    output_parquet_path.split('/')[-1],
    AWS_ACCESS_KEY_ID, AWS_SECRET_ACCESS_KEY)
```

Now, we've finally transformed all the structured, semi-structured, and unstructured data into a single, uniquely addressable data repository in a compressed format. Let's now prepare this data for LLM fine-tuning.

Preparing data

Efficiently handling large datasets is paramount. One of the most effective ways to manage and process such data is through parallel programming environments. Apache Spark stands out as a powerful tool for this purpose, offering robust capabilities for data processing, analysis, and machine learning. Specifically, PySpark, the Python API for Spark, simplifies these tasks with its easy-to-use interface. This section explores how to import collected data, which is stored in Parquet format, into PySpark for parallel processing in an effort to fine-tune the LLM.

PySpark is an interface for Apache Spark, which allows for distributed data processing across clusters. Spark's in-memory computation capabilities make it significantly faster for certain operations compared to other big data technologies. Parquet, on the other hand, is a columnar storage file format that is optimized for use with big data processing frameworks. It offers efficient data compression and encoding schemes, leading to improved performance for complex data processing tasks.

The combination of PySpark and the Parquet format is particularly powerful. It enables the handling of large datasets with improved I/O efficiency, supports sophisticated data analysis pipelines, and facilitates scalable machine learning applications.

Let's look at a script that imports our transformed data into a PySpark cluster:

```python
from pyspark.sql import SparkSession

spark = SparkSession.builder \
    .appName("DataLoadingExample") \
    .getOrCreate()

parquet_file_path = 's3://your-bucket-name/path-to-your-file/data.
parquet'
df = spark.read.parquet(parquet_file_path)

df.show()
```

```
+------------+---------------------------------------------------------
|QuestionID |Question       |Answer         |Context       | ...| +-----------
-+------------+---------------+---------------+-----
|Q000000001 |How can ... |You can r... |Our retu... | ...| +-----------
-+------------+---------------+---------------+-----
|Q000000002 |What is ... |Returns o... |Our retu... | ...| +-----------
-+------------+---------------+---------------+-----
|Q000000003 |How are ... |Next day ... |Shipping... | ...| +-----------
-+------------+---------------+---------------+-----
|Q000000004 |How may ... |Emailing ... |Contact ... | ...| +-----------
-+------------+---------------+---------------+-----
```

Now that we've loaded the data into a PySpark cluster, we can move on to preparing the data for LLM fine-tuning. This involves cleaning, contextual validation, and standard formatting. By leveraging PySpark for these tasks, we can efficiently process large volumes of text data, ensuring that the resulting dataset is primed for maximizing the LLM's learning potential.

Cleaning text data

Text data, especially when extracted from varied sources such as web pages or customer support platforms, often contains inconsistencies, special characters, HTML tags, and other forms of noise that can impede the model's learning process. The first step in preparing the data involves cleaning these elements to ensure uniformity and clarity. Let's look at a Python example of how to do this:

```python
from pyspark.sql import SparkSession
from pyspark.sql.functions import udf, regexp_replace, trim
from pyspark.sql.types import StringType
import re
```

```
spark = SparkSession.builder.appName("Text Cleaning").getOrCreate()

contraction_mapping = {
    "can't": "cannot",
    "won't": "will not",
    "n't": " not",
    "'re": " are",
    "'s": " is",
    "'d": " would",
    "'ll": " will",
    "'t": " not",
    "'ve": " have",
    "'m": " am"
}
```

The preceding code imports the required libraries and also defines the necessary constants to map and remove contractions. Let's now look at how we can use this constant to expand a contraction:

```
def expand_contractions(text, contraction_mapping):
    contractions_pattern = re.compile(
        '({})'.format('|'.join(contraction_mapping.keys())),
        flags=re.IGNORECASE )

    def expand_match(contraction):
        match = contraction.group(0)
        first_char = match[0]
        expanded_contraction = contraction_mapping.get(
            match.lower() if match.lower() in contraction_mapping else
match)
        expanded_contraction = first_char+expanded_contraction[1:]
        return expanded_contraction

    expanded_text = contractions_pattern.sub(expand_match, text)
    return expanded_text

expand_contractions_udf = udf(expand_contractions, StringType())
```

Here, we can see that we can use the contraction map to expand all the contractions to a normalized form. This ensures consistency across the data. Let's now get into the core function of cleaning the text:

```
def clean_text(df):
    # Remove HTML tags
    df = df.withColumn("Question", regexp_replace("Question", "<.*?>",
""))
```

```python
    df = df.withColumn("Answer", regexp_replace("Answer", "<.*?>",
        ""))

    # Remove hyperlinks
    df = df.withColumn("Question", regexp_replace("Question",
        "http[s]?://\S+", ""))
    df = df.withColumn("Answer", regexp_replace("Answer",
        "http[s]?://\S+", ""))

    # Remove special characters
    df = df.withColumn("Question", regexp_replace("Question",
        "[^a-zA-Z0-9\s]", ""))
    df = df.withColumn("Answer", regexp_replace("Answer",
        "[^a-zA-Z0-9\s]", ""))

    # Replace multiple spaces with a single space and trim leading/
trailing spaces
    df = df.withColumn("Question", trim(regexp_replace("Question",
        " +", " ")))
    df = df.withColumn("Answer", trim(regexp_replace("Answer", " +",
        " ")))

    # Expand contractions
    df = df.withColumn("Question",
        expand_contractions_udf("Question"))
    df = df.withColumn("Answer", expand_contractions_udf("Answer"))

    return df
```

Here, we've eliminated HTML tags, unnecessary spaces, special characters, hyperlinks, and contractions to develop a more standardized dataset. Now let's handle the case of limited contexts.

Handling insufficient context

For LLMs to generate meaningful answers, the input data must provide adequate context. Instances lacking this context can lead to vague or irrelevant responses from the model. Identifying and addressing these cases before fine-tuning can significantly enhance the model's effectiveness. Let's review a PySpark function to accomplish this:

```python
from pyspark.sql.functions import when, col, length, size, split
def replace_no_context(df):
    no_context_response = "I don't have enough info to answer this"
    df = df.withColumn("Answer",
                        when((col("Context").isNull()) |
                            (col("Context") == "") |
                            (size(split(col("Context"), " ")) < 3),
```

```
                    no_context_response)
                .otherwise(col("Answer"))))
    return df
```

Now we've made it so that the LLM will let the user know when it doesn't have enough information to confidently answer. Note that this function doesn't account for improperly human-associated Q&A instances and Contexts. Now, let's ensure that the data can be used by the LLM.

Transforming data for LLM consumption

After cleaning the text and addressing instances with insufficient context, the next step involves structuring the data in a format that LLMs can effectively learn from. This typically involves creating a prompt from the question (and optionally the context) and specifying the expected answer:

```
from pyspark.sql.functions import when, col, concat

def format_for_llm_with_labels(df):
    df = df.withColumn(
        "FormattedPrompt",
        when(col("Context") != "",
            concat(
                lit("Context: "), col("Context"),
                lit(" \n\nQuestion: "), col("Question"),
                lit(" \n\nAnswer: "), col("Answer"), lit(" ####")
            )
        ).otherwise(
            concat(
                lit("Question: "), col("Question"),
                lit(" \n\nAnswer: "), col("Answer"), lit(" ####")
            )
        )
    )
    return df.select("FormattedPrompt")

df_formatted_with_labels = format_for_llm_with_labels(df)
```

This function adjustment ensures that each entry in the DataFrame is formatted into a single string under the `FormattedPrompt` column, following the structure in this code block:

```
+------------------------------------------------------------------+
|FormattedPrompt
+------------------------------------------------------------------+
|Context: If you've forgotten your password or wish to |change it for
security reasons, resetting your password is |simple. Follow our step-
by-step guide on the password |reset page.
```

```
|Question: How can I reset my password?
|Answer: To reset your password, navigate to the settings |page,
select 'Password Reset,' and follow the |instructions. ####
+------------------------------------------------------------------
------------------------------------------+
```

The preceding structure shows what will be provided to the model. This format depends on the model specifications and is crucial to ensure consistent outputs. Let's see an example of how to combine the preceding functions into a PySpark job that leverages parallelized compute.

Example Workflow in PySpark

By combining the steps outlined in the preceding section into a PySpark workflow, we can prepare our dataset for LLM fine-tuning as follows:

```
from pyspark.sql import SparkSession

spark = SparkSession.builder.appName("LLM Data Preparation").
getOrCreate()

df = spark.read.parquet("path/to/your/data.parquet")

df_cleaned = clean_text(df)
df_context_handled = replace_no_context(df_cleaned)
df_final = format_for_llm(df_context_handled)

df_final.write.parquet("path/to/your/clean_data_for_llm.parquet",
    mode="overwrite")
```

This code runs the functions we've previously defined. The difference here is that the functions are executed serially across a compute environment that can handle large amounts of data. Let's now look at automating this PySpark job so that it runs periodically without manual intervention.

Automating Spark Jobs

In the world of Unix and Linux, `cron` is a powerful and widely used tool for scheduling tasks to run automatically at fixed times, dates, or intervals. It is particularly useful for automating routine tasks such as backups, updates, and, relevant to our context, running PySpark jobs. Utilizing `cron` to automate the execution of PySpark scripts every 24 hours ensures that data processing workflows are consistently and reliably executed without manual intervention.

At its core, `cron` uses a `cron` table (`crontab`) file, a configuration file that specifies shell commands to run periodically on a given schedule. Each user on a system can have their own `crontab` file, and there's also a system-wide `crontab`.

To edit or create your user's `crontab` file, use the `crontab -e` command in your terminal. If you're using `cron` for the first time, you might be prompted to select an editor.

A `crontab` file consists of lines of six fields. The fields are separated by spaces or tabs, and each field represents a time unit. The syntax is as follows:

```
* * * * * /command/to/execute
```

The fields represent (from left to right) minute (`0 - 59`), hour (`0 - 23`), day of the month (`1 - 31`), month (`1 - 12`), day of the week (`0 - 6`, Sunday being `0`), and the command to run.

To run a PySpark script every 24 hours, you would set the first two fields to specify the time of day when you want the job to run. For example, to run a job at 3:00 AM every day, you would use the following:

```
0 3 * * * /path/to/spark-submit --master local[4] /path/to/your_
pyspark_script.py
```

This line schedules the PySpark script located at `/path/to/your_pyspark_script.py` to run daily at 3:00 AM. Adjust the path to `spark-submit` and adjust your script as necessary. The `--master local [4]` option tells Spark to run locally using four cores. Adjust this according to your environment and needs.

After adding the line for your PySpark job, save and close the editor. The `cron` daemon will automatically install the new `crontab`, and your PySpark job is now scheduled to run every 24 hours.

Ensuring the reliability of automated PySpark jobs scheduled with `cron` requires monitoring and alerting. Let's go over a few approaches to achieve this, enabling swift detection and response to any operational anomalies.

Direct the standard output (`stdout`) and standard error (`stderr`) of your PySpark job to separate log files:

```
0 3 * * * /path/to/spark-submit /path/to/your_script.py >> /path/to/
output.log 2>> /path/to/error.log
```

This setup ensures that all outputs and errors are captured for analysis. Tools such as Prometheus or the ELK Stack can ingest these logs, allowing for real-time monitoring. Alternatively, a custom script can periodically check for new entries in the error log.

Based on the monitoring setup, you can configure alerts to notify you or your team of any issues detected. Alerts can be configured to send notifications through various channels, including the following:

- **Email**: Utilize tools such as Logwatch for sending email notifications based on log file entries

- **SMS and messaging apps**: Integrate with services such as Twilio or platforms such as Slack to receive immediate alerts

- **Incident management tools**: Connect with tools such as PagerDuty through webhooks for a sophisticated incident response approach

A bash script can serve as a simple alerting mechanism, checking the error log for new entries and sending an email alert if errors are found:

```bash
#!/bin/bash
if [[ -s /path/to/error.log ]]; then
    mail -s "PySpark Job Error Detected" user@example.com < /path/to/
error.log
    # Clear the log file after sending the alert
    > /path/to/error.log
fi
```

This script, scheduled to run after the PySpark job, offers a straightforward way to stay informed about job failures.

Summary

This chapter covered the comprehensive process of handling textual data for LLM applications, starting from the collection of data across diverse sources and progressing to the transformation of this data into a structured format that is conducive to analysis and model training. It further explored the preparation phase, wherein data is imported into parallel programming environments for cleansing and standardization, enhancing its quality for LLM fine-tuning. Lastly, it emphasized the importance of automation in streamlining these processes, ensuring both efficiency and consistency in preparing high-quality datasets for advanced language model applications. In the next chapter, we'll cover LLM development and fine-tuning.

4

Developing Models via LLMOps

In this chapter, we'll cover how to develop a **large language models** (LLM) while ensuring that LLMOps best practices are followed. This ensures that the developed LLM can be effectively reviewed and eventually deployed to production. The information in this chapter exemplifies a real-world use case for developing a performant LLM through LLMOps. We will be looking at the following topics:

- Creating features

- Storing features

- Retrieving features

- Selecting foundation models

- Fine-tuning models

- Tuning hyperparameters

- Automating model development

Creating features

Features are derived from processed data typically used as input to models. Creating features in a distributed computing environment is fundamental to developing scalable machine learning models. Utilizing distributed computing frameworks, such as PySpark, allows for the efficient processing and engineering of features from vast datasets, ensuring the data is adequately prepared and optimized for model training. This process not only streamlines the preparation of large-scale data but also enhances the quality of features fed into machine learning algorithms, crucial for building robust and accurate models. Let's look at creating features from the formatted text that we produced last chapter:

```
+-----------------------------------------------------------------------
-------------------------------------------------+
|FormattedPrompt
+-----------------------------------------------------------------------
-------------------------------------------------+
```

```
|Context: If you've forgotten your password or wish to change it for
security                        |reasons, resetting your password is
simple. Follow our step-by-step guide on the
|password reset page.
|Question: How can I reset my password?
|Answer: To reset your password, navigate to the settings page, select
'Password Reset,' |and follow the instructions. ####
+-------------------------------------------------------------------
---------------------------------------+
```

Let's examine the script that first creates a new column in a DataFrame to represent the annotated sections from the preceding format. This will help us eventually create features to be used in model fine-tuning:

```python
from pyspark.sql import SparkSession
from pyspark.sql.functions import split
from pyspark.sql.functions import udf
from pyspark.sql.types import MapType, StringType

spark = SparkSession.builder \
    .appName("Annotation and Alignment") \
    .getOrCreate()

data = [
    ("Context: If you've forgotten your password or wish to change
it for security reasons, resetting your password is simple. Follow
our step-by-step guide on the password reset page. Question: How can
I reset my password? Answer: To reset your password, navigate to the
settings page, select 'Password Reset,' and follow the instructions.
####",)
]

columns = ["FormattedPrompt"]
df = spark.createDataFrame(data, schema=columns)
```

The preceding code defines the imports, the sample data, and Spark DataFrame creation with a single column. Next, let's define some core functions:

```python
def extract_sections(formatted_prompt):
    split_prompt = formatted_prompt.split(" Question: ")
    context_part = split_prompt[0].replace("Context: ", "")
    question_answer = split_prompt[1].split(" Answer: ")
    question_part = question_answer[0]
    answer_part = question_answer[1].split(" ####")[0]
```

```
    return {
        "context": context_part,
        "question": question_part,
        "answer": answer_part
    }


extract_sections_udf = udf(extract_sections,
    MapType(StringType(), StringType()))


annotated_df = df.withColumn("AnnotatedSections",
    extract_sections_udf(df["FormattedPrompt"]))


annotated_df.select("AnnotatedSections").show(truncate=False)


spark.stop()
```

The script initializes a PySpark session and creates a sample DataFrame to replicate the provided input structure. It then defines a function, `extract_sections`, designed to parse the formatted prompt into distinct sections for context, question, and answer, and returns these components as a dictionary. This function is registered as a **User-Defined Function (UDF)** within PySpark, allowing it to be applied across the DataFrame. Consequently, a new column, `AnnotatedSections`, is created, showcasing the structured dictionary for each row. Here's an example of the output:

```
annotated_prompt = {
    "context": "If you've forgotten your password or wish to change
it for security reasons, resetting your password is simple. Follow our
step-by-step guide on the password reset page.",
    "question": "How can I reset my password?",
    "answer": "To reset your password, navigate to the settings page,
select 'Password Reset,' and follow the instructions."
}
```

Here we see the transformed dataframe, illustrating the successful annotation and alignment of the original text data into a more structured format. Having transformed the original data into a structured format with annotated sections for context, question, and answer, we now transition to the tokenization stage. The next step involves converting the text from each section into a sequence of tokens, which will enable subsequent processing by machine learning models in a format they can understand and analyze effectively.

Tokenizing annotations

Tokenizing the annotated section is a crucial step that enables the model to assign unique IDs to each token and utilize attention masks. These elements are essential for improving the performance and computational efficiency of the mathematical operations involved in training and making predictions with LLMs. To accurately interpret and process input data, models rely on tokenizers that break text into manageable pieces. A simple word tokenizer splits text into individual words, which is straightforward and easy to implement but struggles with **Out-of-Vocabulary** (**OOV**) words and lacks subword information. In contrast, trained subword tokenizers, such as **Byte Pair Encoding** (**BPE**) or **WordPiece**, segment text into subwords based on frequency in a training corpus. This approach handles rare and compound words better, captures morphological information, and enhances the model's generalization across different languages and domains. While more complex to implement, trained subword tokenizers significantly improve the model's learning and inference capabilities by providing richer and more flexible text representations.

Let's continue the previous example by now tokenizing the annotated data for the Llama2 foundation model to get a better understanding of what's happening:

```python
from pyspark.sql import SparkSession
from pyspark.sql.functions import udf, col
from pyspark.sql.types import ArrayType, StringType
from transformers import AutoTokenizer


spark = SparkSession.builder.appName
    ("LLaMA Tokenization").getOrCreate()
tokenizer = AutoTokenizer.from_pretrained("Llama2-tokenizer",
    use_fast=True)


@udf(returnType=ArrayType(StringType()))
def tokenize_text(text):
    tokens = tokenizer.tokenize(text)
    return tokens


tokenized_df = annotated_df.withColumn("tokens",
    tokenize_text(col("AnnotatedSections")))


spark.stop()
```

The preceding coding example demonstrates how to integrate a tokenizer from the `transformers` library with PySpark for distributed processing, specifically focusing on tokenizing text data within a PySpark DataFrame. Here's an example row output of the preceding function:

```
| tokens                                                              |
-----------------------------------------------------------------------
```

```
| ['context', ':', 'if', 'you', "'", 've', 'forgotten', 'your',
'password', 'or', 'wish', 'to', 'change', 'it', 'for', 'security',
'reasons', ',', 'resetting', 'your', 'password', 'is', 'simple', '.',
'follow', 'our', 'step', '-', 'by', '-', 'step', 'guide', 'on', 'the',
'password', 'reset', 'page', '.', 'question', ':', 'how', 'can', 'i',
'reset', 'my', 'password', '?', 'answer', ':', 'to', 'reset', 'your',
'password', ',', 'navigate', 'to', 'the', 'settings', 'page', ',',
'select', "'", 'password' ...    |
```

To maximize computational efficiency, each token is assigned a numerical ID, allowing models to process numbers instead of text. Vocabulary size and OOV handling are crucial: a larger vocabulary captures more nuances but requires more resources, while a smaller one is more efficient but struggles with rare words. Trained subword tokenizers such as BPE or WordPiece handle OOV words by breaking them into smaller, recognizable subwords. For example, using the BERT tokenizer from the Hugging Face Transformers library, the text is tokenized into subwords and converted into numerical IDs, which the model processes efficiently. This approach ensures that even unknown words can be partially understood and handled, optimizing the performance of LLMs.

Uniquely identifying tokens with attention masks

Unique IDs convert text into numerical representations, and attention masks identify relevant tokens for the model's focus, distinguishing meaningful content from padding—extra, non-informative tokens added to ensure uniform length across data inputs. Padding is essential because machine learning models require inputs of consistent size for structured processing and efficient batch operations. This combination of unique IDs, attention masks, and padding, especially when implemented in scalable environments such as PySpark, allows for the efficient handling of large datasets. It ensures that models focus computational resources on pertinent content, enhancing processing accuracy and streamlining the training and inference phases by maintaining data uniformity.

Here's a code example of how to use PySpark to implement numerical representations, attention masking, and padding:

```python
from pyspark.sql import SparkSession
from pyspark.sql.functions import udf
from pyspark.sql.types import (
    ArrayType, IntegerType, StructType, StructField)
import torch
```

Now that we've established the preceding import, let's initialize the Spark session, dataframe, and a function:

```python
spark = SparkSession.builder.appName("Token IDs and Attention Masks").
getOrCreate()


df = spark.createDataFrame(data, ["tokens"])
```

```python
def tokens_to_ids_attention_mask(tokens):
    tokens = tokenizer.tokenize(tokens)
    inputs = tokenizer(tokens, truncation=True, padding='max_length',
    max_length=512, return_tensors="pt")
    token_ids = inputs['input_ids'].tolist()[0]  # Convert to list for
Spark compatibility
    attention_mask = inputs['attention_mask'].tolist()[0]
    return (token_ids, attention_mask)
```

Now we can carry on the core of the code to transform the data:

```python
schema = StructType([
    StructField("token_ids", ArrayType(IntegerType()), False),
    StructField("attention_mask", ArrayType(IntegerType()), False)
])

tokens_to_ids_attention_mask_udf = udf(tokens_to_ids_attention_mask,
    schema)

df_with_ids_masks = df.withColumn("ids_masks",
    tokens_to_ids_attention_mask_udf(df["tokens"]))

df_final = df_with_ids_masks.select("tokens",
    "ids_masks.token_ids", "ids_masks.attention_mask")

df_final.show(truncate=False)

spark.stop()
```

This code is a PySpark job that transforms a DataFrame containing pre-tokenized text in a column named `tokens` by applying a UDF to generate token IDs and attention masks for each row. The UDF, `tokens_to_ids_attention_mask`, leverages a tokenizer (assumed to be previously defined and loaded) to convert the text tokens into their corresponding numerical IDs and attention masks (suitable for input into Transformer-based models) and then adds these as new columns to the DataFrame.

Here's an example of the output of this script:

```
|tokens          |token_ids            |attention_mask        |    +----------
--+--------------------+---------------------+
|["context",     |[101, 9530, 2065,    |[1, 1, 1, 1, 0, ... ]|
```

The table displays truncated versions of the `tokens`, `token_ids`, and `attention_mask` columns, demonstrating the resulting data structure of the processed annotations.

Now that we have the text data transformed into features that the model requires, let's store these elements in a **Feast feature** store.

Storing features

Feature stores are essential in providing a centralized platform for the management, storage, and serving of engineered features across multiple machine learning projects. They play a crucial role in enhancing consistency, reducing redundancy, and accelerating the model development and deployment process. By organizing and making features readily accessible, feature stores such as Feast ensure that LLMOps best practices are followed by efficiently retrieving and utilizing preprocessed features for LLM training, thereby streamlining the machine learning workflow and supporting scalable solutions.

Let's look at an example for storing data related to `tokens`, `token_ids`, and `attention_mask` in Feast. This involves creating a new Feast project to accommodate the storage of tokenized text data and its associated metadata for LLM training and inference:

```
feast init token_feast_project
cd token_feast_project
```

If you haven't already, save your PySpark dataframe containing the processed annotations to S3. This makes the data available to Feast for ingestion:

```
from pyspark.sql import SparkSession
spark = SparkSession.builder \
    .appName("Save DataFrame to S3") \
    .config("spark.jars.packages",
        "org.apache.hadoop:hadoop-aws:3.2.0") \
    .getOrCreate()

df = spark.createDataFrame(data, schema=columns)
s3_path = "s3://your-bucket-name/your-path/spark_processed_data.csv"
df.write.csv(s3_path, mode="overwrite", header=True)
spark.stop()
```

Now that we have the tokens, token IDs, and attention masks saved to S3, we can execute the following `features.py` script, which configures how Feast should interpret the data at the configured source, including which columns represent entities, features, timestamps, and so on:

```
from feast import Entity, Feature, FeatureView, ValueType
from feast.data_source import FileSource
from datetime import datetime

input_data_source = FileSource(
    path="s3://your-bucket-name/your-path/spark_processed_data.csv",
    timestamp_field="event_timestamp",
    created_timestamp_column="created_timestamp",
)
```

```
input_entity = Entity(name="input_id", value_type=ValueType.STRING,
    description="Unique ID for the input")

token_features_fv = FeatureView(
    name="token_features_view",
    entities=["input_id"],
    ttl=datetime.timedelta(days=1),
    features=[
        Feature(name="tokens", dtype=ValueType.STRING_LIST),
        Feature(name="token_ids", dtype=ValueType.INT64_LIST),
        Feature(name="attention_mask", dtype=ValueType.INT64_LIST),
    ],
    batch_source=input_data_source,
)
```

Next, we run `feast apply` to register these feature definitions and data source configurations with the Feast registry, updating Feast's understanding of what features are available and how to access them.

Finally, we need to materialize the historical data to officially ingest the processed annotations into Feast. Materializing historical data within the context of Feast ensures that the prepared feature data is systematically stored and made accessible for subsequent LLM training or inference. Historical data encompasses all the feature information that has been accumulated up to the present moment. The term *historical* underscores the data's applicability for backward-looking analyses and model development, setting it apart from real-time or future-oriented data streams that might be utilized for immediate predictions.

The `feature_store.yaml` file in your Feast project directory configures how and where your data is materialized. The following is an example configuration that specifies both online and offline storage destinations:

```
project: my_feast_project
registry: s3://my-feast-bucket/registry.db
provider: aws
online_store:
    type: dynamodb
    region: us-west-2
offline_store:
    type: s3
    s3_endpoint_url: s3.amazonaws.com
    path: s3://my-feast-bucket/raw_data/
```

In the preceding configuration, `project` names the project, while `registry` specifies an S3 location for storing Feast's metadata. The `provider` instance is set to `aws`, indicating the use of AWS services. The `online_store` instance is configured to use Amazon **DynamoDB** for low-latency feature serving, with a specified region for the DynamoDB tables. The `offline_store` instance is set to use S3, detailing the bucket (and, optionally, a path within it) for storing batch data, facilitating the integration of cloud-native storage solutions for both online and offline feature management in Feast.

Online storage, optimized for low-latency access, facilitates real-time model predictions by allowing models to swiftly query the latest feature values for given entities. This setup is paramount in production environments where the speed of prediction is critical. Conversely, offline storage caters to scalability and cost-efficiency, making it more suitable for training models across expansive datasets.

Now that we have `feature_store.yaml` configured for S3, you can materialize data into the online store using the `feast materialize-incremental` command. This command reads the latest feature data up to the specified timestamp from your S3 bucket and loads it into the configured online store for serving:

```
feast materialize-incremental $(date -u +"%Y-%m-%dT%H:%M:%S")
```

This command incrementally updates the online store with the latest historical data from the S3 batch source up to the current UTC timestamp, ensuring the online store remains current with all available data. Now, we can retrieve these features for use in analysis, training, or evaluation.

Retrieving features

Let's explore how to retrieve tokenized data, including `tokens`, `token_ids`, and `attention_mask`, from Feast for use with an LLM. The process differs slightly depending on whether we're accessing features for real-time predictions (online) or training machine learning models (offline). Here's how we'll approach both scenarios:

```python
from datetime import datetime
from feast import FeatureStore
import pandas as pd
fs = FeatureStore(repo_path="/path/to/your/feast_project")
feature_refs = [
    "token_features_view:tokens",
    "token_features_view:token_ids",
    "token_features_view:attention_mask",
]

entity_keys = [{"input_id": "1"}, {"input_id": "2"}]

online_features = fs.get_online_features(
    entity_rows=entity_keys,
```

```
        feature_refs=feature_refs,
).to_dict()

entity_df = pd.DataFrame({
    "input_id": ["1", "2", "3"],
    "event_timestamp": pd.to_datetime(["2022-01-01",
        "2022-01-02", "2022-01-03"]),
})

historical_features = fs.get_historical_features(
    entity_df=entity_df,
    feature_refs=feature_refs,
).to_df()
```

This script uses Feast to retrieve features in both online and offline contexts.

Online feature retrieval, aimed at real-time applications, fetches the latest feature values for specified entities from an online feature store, which requires a low-latency database such as **Redis** or **DynamoDB**. We defined this earlier in `feature_store.yaml`:

```
online_store:
    type: dynamodb
    region: us-west-2
```

Conversely, offline feature retrieval is used in training scenarios by accessing historical data over specific timeframes from an offline store, including data warehouses or lakes, such as BigQuery or Amazon S3. We also defined this earlier in `feature_store.yaml`:

```
offline_store:
    type: s3
    s3_endpoint_url: s3.amazonaws.com
    path: s3://my-feast-offline-bucket/raw_data/
```

The choice between online and offline retrieval hinges on the application's needs: online retrieval for immediate predictions and offline for model training or batch analysis. This delineation ensures that the infrastructure—whether for low-latency access in production environments or for comprehensive historical data analysis—supports the distinct requirements of online serving and offline training effectively.

Now that we have a feature store with all of our training and fine-tuning data available in online and offline stores, we can move on to selecting the right foundation model, also referred to as a pretrained LLM. By storing the tokens in the feature store, we can reprocess the unique IDs and attention mechanisms based on the selected foundation model, including Llama 2, Gemma, or Mixtral.

Selecting the foundation model

Selecting the right foundation model for your text generation task is a pivotal decision that shapes the capabilities, efficiency, and scalability of your LLM application. With the advent of models like Mistral, Llama2, and Gemma, the landscape of foundation models has expanded, offering tailored solutions for a wide array of applications.

This section explores the considerations for choosing between these cutting-edge models.

Choosing the LLM for your specific use case

The foundational step in leveraging AI for any task is to precisely define the desired outcome. This clarity is crucial as it directly influences the selection of an appropriate AI model by pinpointing the exact features needed for success, including nuanced language comprehension, creative output generation, and the ability to personalize content. By focusing on models available on platforms such as Hugging Face that are pre-aligned with these specific requirements, this step ensures a targeted approach in choosing a model. It facilitates the exploration of models that have been pretrained or fine-tuned with capabilities closely matching the project's goals, streamlining the process of finding an AI solution that can adeptly fulfill the outlined objectives.

For our website's Q&A application, where the primary goal is to deliver prompt and accurate answers to user queries, utilizing pre-tuned question-answering LLMs ensures that the system is well-equipped to meet user expectations right from the outset. We can browse the most performant open source models using *Papers With Code* and explore the **Question Answering** benchmarks and datasets. Refer to the following screenshot:

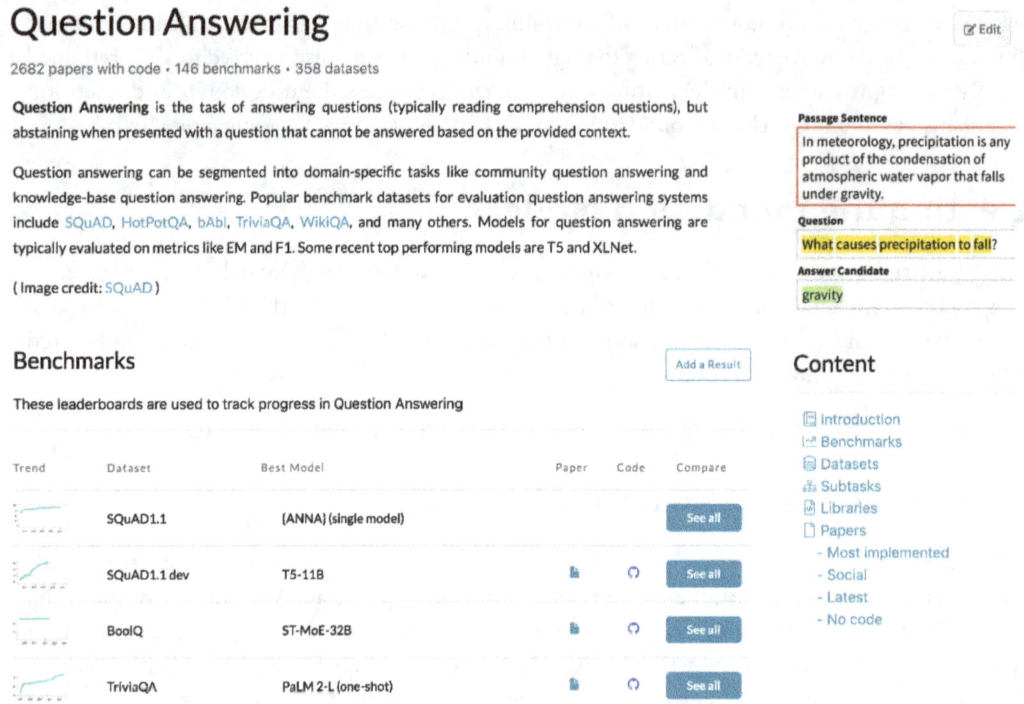

Figure 4.1 – Papers With Code – Question Answering leaderboard

The preceding screenshot indicates which open source models perform best against particular **Question Answering (QA)** datasets. Let's select **T5-11B** since it's accompanied by a paper and downloadable code hosted on GitHub. When selecting the T5-11B model for a QA task, several key factors need consideration: its large size of 11 billion parameters requires substantial computational resources, and its inference speed can be slow, necessitating powerful GPUs or TPUs for efficient processing. T5-11B is a general-purpose model trained on diverse tasks, but fine-tuning on your specific QA dataset is crucial if your subtask differs significantly from its original training data. Despite these challenges, the model's versatility, along with its accompanying paper and downloadable code on GitHub, make it a strong candidate for high-performance QA applications.

The **Text-to-Text Transfer Transformer** (T5) model uses an encoder to transform input data into a context-rich representation, which the decoder then uses to generate the output. T5 is pretrained on a mix of unsupervised and supervised tasks and shows versatility across various tasks by merely prefixing the input with the task's name, such as `translate...` for translations or `summarize...` for summarizations. For our use case, we'll provide context, a question, and an answer when fine-tuning. Now that we have a model selected, let's test it out on an example.

Testing foundation LLMs

We'll use the p3.8xlarge or p3.16xlarge AWS instances; these offer multiple **NVIDIA Tesla V100 GPUs** to run the following example script, which helps us understand the applicability of the foundation model to our use case. Using our previous work on Feast, we can run inference on a stored training example:

```
from transformers import T5Tokenizer, T5ForConditionalGeneration
from feast import FeatureStore
import pandas as pd

fs = FeatureStore(repo_path="/path/to/your/feast_project")

feature_refs = [
    "qa_features_view:context",
    "qa_features_view:question",
]

entity_df = pd.DataFrame({
    "entity_id": [1],   # Example entity ID
    "event_timestamp": pd.to_datetime(["2022-01-01"]),})

historical_features = fs.get_historical_features(
    entity_df=entity_df,
    feature_refs=feature_refs,
).to_df()

context = historical_features["qa_features_view:context"].iloc[0]
question = historical_features["qa_features_view:question"].iloc[0]

tokenizer = T5Tokenizer.from_pretrained("t5-small")
model = T5ForConditionalGeneration.from_pretrained("t5-small")

input_text = f"question: {question} context: {context}"
input_ids = tokenizer(input_text, return_tensors="pt").input_ids

outputs = model.generate(input_ids)
answer = tokenizer.decode(outputs[0], skip_special_tokens=True)
```

The preceding code retrieves specific question and context data from a Feast feature store and employs the T5 model to generate an answer. It fetches historical features for a question and its context, formats this information for the T5 model, and then decodes the model's generated response into a readable answer, demonstrating the integration of feature storage with NLP model inference.

Let's assume that the features of the tokens fetched are as follows:

```
+-------------------------------------------------------------------------
------------------------------------------------+

|FormattedPrompt

+-------------------------------------------------------------------------
------------------------------------------------+

|Context: If you've forgotten your password or wish to change it for
security                        |reasons, resetting your password is
simple. Follow our step-by-step guide on the
|password reset page.
|Question: How can I reset my password?
|Answer: To reset your password, navigate to the settings page, select
'Password Reset,' |and follow the instructions. ####

+-------------------------------------------------------------------------
------------------------------------------------+
```

Let's also assume that the answer produced by the T5 LLM is the following:

```
Navigate to the settings page, select 'Password Reset,' and follow the
instructions.
```

This shows we're on the right track by selecting this LLM and can further evaluate this model for our use case.

Addressing additional model concerns

It's important to address all concerns when selecting the foundation LLM to ensure the successful integration of AI capabilities into applications. These concerns extend beyond the initial model performance to include latency, size, cost, licensing, and the degree of openness. Each of these factors plays a significant role in the overall feasibility, sustainability, and impact of leveraging a particular model.

Latency refers to the time it takes for a model to process input and generate an output. It is a critical consideration for real-time applications, where responses are expected instantly or within a few milliseconds. High latency can degrade the user experience, making it essential to assess and optimize the inference time. Factors influencing latency include the model's complexity, the hardware used for inference, and the efficiency of the implementation. Models with billions of parameters, while powerful, often suffer from higher latency, prompting the need for model distillation or the selection of smaller, more efficient models for latency-sensitive applications.

The size of a model, often correlated with its parameter count, directly impacts its memory footprint and storage requirements. Larger models demand more storage space and higher memory during inference, which can limit their deployment on edge devices or environments with strict resource constraints. The model size also affects loading times and can contribute to increased latency. Balancing model size with performance needs is essential, particularly when deploying models in resource-constrained environments. Larger models require more computational power and, consequently, incur higher costs.

It's important to consider the total cost of ownership, including the costs of updates, maintenance, and any required scalability to meet user demand.

The licensing of a model determines how it can be used, modified, and distributed. Open source models offer the flexibility to adapt the model to specific needs, contribute to its development, and, potentially, reduce costs associated with proprietary models. However, the degree of openness varies; some models are fully open source, providing access to both the code and the trained weights, while others might only offer binary files without the ability to modify the model architecture or training procedure. Understanding the licensing agreements is crucial to ensure compliance and avoid legal issues, especially for commercial applications. Now that we've covered those concerns, let's move on to model fine-tuning.

Fine-tuning the foundation LLM

Foundation model fine-tuning is crucial as it adapts the model's generalized knowledge to the specific nuances and requirements of a particular task or domain, significantly enhancing its performance and relevance. For a web page Q&A application, fine-tuning a foundation model on domain-specific data ensures that the generated answers are more accurate, contextually appropriate, and tailored to the unique content and user queries associated with the website. Let's review the code that fine-tunes our T5 model with some examples from Feast:

```python
from transformers import T5Tokenizer, T5ForConditionalGeneration
from feast import FeatureStore
import pandas as pd
import torch

fs = FeatureStore(repo_path="/path/to/your/feast_project")

entity_df = pd.DataFrame({
    "entity_id": [1, 2],
    "event_timestamp": pd.to_datetime(["2022-01-01", "2022-01-02"]),
})
feature_refs = ["qa_pairs_view:question", "qa_pairs_view:answer"]
historical_features = fs.get_historical_features(
    entity_df=entity_df, feature_refs=feature_refs
).to_df()

questions = historical_features["qa_pairs_view:question"].tolist()
answers = historical_features["qa_pairs_view:answer"].tolist()
```

Now that we've defined our imports, feature store, and other items, let's move on the tokenization:

```python
tokenizer = T5Tokenizer.from_pretrained("t5-11b")
model = T5ForConditionalGeneration.from_pretrained("t5-11b")


max_source_length = 512
max_target_length = 128


task_prefix = "answer the question: "
input_sequences = [task_prefix + question for question in questions]


encoding = tokenizer(
    input_sequences,
    padding="longest",
    max_length=max_source_length,
    truncation=True,
    return_tensors="pt",
)
```

Now that we've defined our encoding, we can use it to define the rest of our requirements:

```python
input_ids, attention_mask = encoding.input_ids, encoding.attention_
mask

target_encoding = tokenizer(
    answers,
    padding="longest",
    max_length=max_target_length,
    truncation=True,
    return_tensors="pt",
)
labels = target_encoding.input_ids

labels[labels == tokenizer.pad_token_id] = -100

loss = model(input_ids=input_ids, attention_mask=attention_mask,
    labels=labels).loss
print(f"Fine-tuning loss: {loss.item()}")
```

The preceding script begins by retrieving question-answer pairs from the Feast feature store, which are then used as the input and target sequences for fine-tuning the T5 model on a Q&A task. The process involves encoding both the questions (prepended with a task-specific prefix) and the answers, computing the loss with a forward pass, and using this loss to guide the fine-tuning process. This method allows for the model to learn from the specific types of questions and answers encountered in your web page Q&A application, optimizing its ability to generate accurate and relevant answers.

Now that we've fine-tuned the LLM, let's save it to a model store. This is essential to avoid retuning for similar future tasks, ensuring efficient use of resources. A model store, such as Hugging Face, provides a centralized platform for secure model versioning and storage, facilitating easy access and sharing. Utilizing Hugging Face for storing our fine-tuned LLM allows for straightforward integration into LLM workflows, supporting both collaboration and deployment efforts efficiently.

Here is the code for it:

```
from huggingface_hub import HfFolder, Repository

token = HfFolder.get_token()
if token is None:
    raise ValueError("You must be logged into the Hugging Face CLI")

repo_name = "my-private-t5-11b"
repo_path = os.path.join("./", repo_name)
repo = Repository(repo_path, clone_from=f"{repo_name}",
    use_auth_token=True)

model.save_pretrained(repo_path)
tokenizer.save_pretrained(repo_path)

repo.push_to_hub(commit_message="Upload fine-tuned T5 model")
```

This script logs in to Hugging Face, clones a specified repository, and saves a fine-tuned T5 model and its tokenizer to this repository. It then pushes the saved model and tokenizer back to Hugging Face with a commit message, effectively uploading the fine-tuned assets for future access or sharing.

Now that we've saved the model, let's pull it from the repository and requery it to get an understanding of its new performance:

```
from transformers import T5Tokenizer, T5ForConditionalGeneration
from feast import FeatureStore
import pandas as pd

fs = FeatureStore(repo_path="/path/to/your/feast_project")
feature_refs = [
    "qa_data_view:question",
    "qa_data_view:context",
]
entity_df = pd.DataFrame({
    "entity_id": [1],  # Example entity ID for which to fetch data
```

```python
    "event_timestamp": pd.to_datetime(["2022-01-01"]),
})


historical_features = fs.get_historical_features(
    entity_df=entity_df,
    feature_refs=feature_refs,
).to_df()


question = historical_features["qa_data_view:question"].iloc[0]
context = historical_features["qa_data_view:context"].iloc[0]


model_repo = "your_username/my-private-t5-model"


tokenizer = T5Tokenizer.from_pretrained(model_repo)
model = T5ForConditionalGeneration.from_pretrained(model_repo)


input_text = f"question: {question} context: {context}"


input_ids = tokenizer(input_text, return_tensors="pt").input_ids


outputs = model.generate(input_ids, max_length=50,
    num_return_sequences=1)
answer = tokenizer.decode(outputs[0], skip_special_tokens=True)
```

This script fetches question and context data from our Feast feature store and then uses the fine-tuned T5 model from a Hugging Face repository to generate an answer based on the retrieved data.

Here's our new output after fine-tuning with the following context, question, and human-labeled answer:

```
+----------------------------------------------------------------------
--------------------------------------------------+
|FormattedPrompt
+----------------------------------------------------------------------
--------------------------------------------------+
|Context: If you've forgotten your password or wish to change it for
security                     |reasons, resetting your password is
simple. Follow our step-by-step guide on the
|password reset page.
|Question: How can I reset my password?
|Answer: To reset your password, navigate to the settings page, select
'Password Reset,' |and follow the instructions. ####
+----------------------------------------------------------------------
--------------------------------------------------+
```

The answer produced by the fine-tuned T5 LLM is as follows:

```
To reset your password, navigate to the settings page, select
'Password Reset,' and follow the password reset instructions.
```

We can see that the answer does now more closely resemble the expected answer assigned by the human labelers.

Now that we've fine-tuned the model, let's review the hyperparameters we can tune, based on the model, to further improve the performance of the model.

Tuning hyperparameters

Tuning hyperparameters for the **T5** model significantly influences its performance on tasks such as web page Q&A, directly affecting how accurately and efficiently the model generates responses. Hyperparameter optimization involves adjusting various parameters that control the model's training process and architecture to improve its ability to learn and generalize from the training data.

Here's a list of all the available hyperparameters for the T5 LLM:

- `adam_epsilon`: This parameter is related to the epsilon value in the Adam optimizer, which prevents division by zero during the optimization process. A typical value is `1e-08`.

- `cosine_schedule_num_cycles`: In a cosine annealing learning rate schedule, this value, set at `0.5`, represents the number of cycles during training.

- `do_lower_case`: A Boolean indicating whether to convert all letters to lowercase during tokenization. For T5, this is typically set to `False`.

- `early_stopping_consider_epochs`: A Boolean to determine whether early stopping should consider epochs. It is set as `False` here.

- `early_stopping_metric`: Specifies the metric to monitor for early stopping; `eval_loss` is commonly used.

- `early_stopping_metric_minimize`: This Boolean value, set to `True`, indicates that the training process should aim to minimize the metric specified for early stopping.

- `early_stopping_patience`: Refers to the number of evaluations to wait for improvement before early stopping. Here, it is set to `2`.

- `adafactor_eps`: This set of two values, (`1e-30` and `0.001`), specifies the epsilon values used in the Adafactor optimizer to maintain numerical stability.

- `adafactor_clip_threshold`: Set to `1.0`, this parameter is the clipping threshold for gradients when using the Adafactor optimizer.

- `adafactor_decay_rate`: Represents the decay rate of the second moment estimator in the Adafactor optimizer, set to `-0.8` here.

- `adafactor_scale_parameter`: A Boolean indicating whether to scale the learning rate in the Adafactor optimizer, set to `False` in this case.

- `adafactor_relative_step`: Another Boolean specifying whether the Adafactor optimizer should use a relative step size, also `False` here.

- `adafactor_warmup_init`: Set to `False`, indicating that the Adafactor optimizer should not use a warmup initialization.

The `adam_epsilon` hyperparameter helps maintain numerical stability during the optimization process. If this value is set too high, the optimizer might become too conservative, potentially leading to slower convergence or suboptimal solutions:

```
Higher adam_epsilon (1e-02):
Input: "What methods of payment do you accept?"
Output: "We accept many payment methods."
Optimal adam_epsilon (1e-08):
Output: "We accept credit cards, PayPal, and bank transfers."
```

The `early_stopping_patience` hyperparameter determines how many evaluations to wait for an improvement in the monitored metric before stopping training early. Setting this too low may result in premature stopping, while too high a value can lead to overfitting:

```
Low early_stopping_patience (100):
Input: "Can I change my booking date?"
Output: "Booking changes are subject."
Higher early_stopping_patience (1000):
Output: "You can change your booking date up to 24 hours before the
scheduled time without any additional fee."
```

The `adafactor_decay_rate` hyperparameter influences how quickly the learning rates decay over time. A negative decay rate can lead to an increase in learning rates, which might not be suitable for all training stages:

```
Negative adafactor_decay_rate (-0.8):
Input: "How long is the warranty period?"
Output: "Warranty varies."
Positive adafactor_decay_rate (1e-01):
Output: "The warranty period for our products is one year from the
date of purchase."
cosine_schedule_num_cycles
```

Adjusting these hyperparameters requires careful monitoring of model performance on a validation set to ensure that the changes lead to improved accuracy and generalization, rather than overfitting or underfitting. Fine-tuning these settings is a delicate process that can significantly affect the model's ability to provide precise and informative answers in a web page Q&A setting.

Hyperparameter tuning techniques often involve methods such as grid search, random search, Bayesian optimization, or using automated machine learning tools such as Hyperopt and Optuna, which can systematically explore the hyperparameter space to find the optimal configuration. Tools such as **Weights & Biases** and MLflow can track experiments and facilitate this process by visualizing the effects of different hyperparameters on model performance, aiding in the selection of the best set of hyperparameters for a given task.

Hyperopt is a Python library for hyperparameter tuning that uses Bayesian optimization for efficient search across high-dimensional and complex hyperparameter spaces. Let's use Hyperopt to tune hyperparameters for us:

```python
from hyperopt import hp, fmin, tpe, STATUS_OK, Trials
from transformers import(
    T5Tokenizer, T5ForConditionalGeneration,
    Trainer, TrainingArguments)
from datasets import load_dataset

space = {
    'learning_rate': hp.loguniform('learning_rate', -7, -2),
    'per_device_train_batch_size': hp.choice(
        'per_device_train_batch_size', [8, 16, 32, 64]),
    'num_train_epochs': hp.choice('num_train_epochs', [2, 3, 4]),
    'weight_decay': hp.uniform('weight_decay', 0.0, 0.3),
}
```

Now that we've defined our imports and search space, let's move on to defining the functions:

```python
def objective(hyperparams):
    tokenizer = T5Tokenizer.from_pretrained("/path/to/fine-tuned")
    model = T5ForConditionalGeneration.from_pretrained(
        "/path/to/fine-tuned")
    training_args = TrainingArguments(
        output_dir="your-model",
        learning_rate=hyperparams['learning_rate'],
        per_device_train_batch_size=hyperparams[
            'per_device_train_batch_size'],
        num_train_epochs=hyperparams['num_train_epochs'],
        weight_decay=hyperparams['weight_decay'],
        evaluation_strategy="epoch",
        save_strategy="epoch",
        load_best_model_at_end=True,
        push_to_hub=False,
    )

    trainer = Trainer(
```

```
        model=model,
        args=training_args,
        train_dataset=dataset["train"],
        eval_dataset=dataset["validation"],
    )
```

Now, we can use the functions to train and evaluate the model:

```
    trainer.train()
    eval_results = trainer.evaluate()

    return {'loss': eval_results["eval_loss"], 'status': STATUS_OK}

best = fmin(
    fn=objective,
    space=space,
    algo=tpe.suggest,
    max_evals=3,
    trials=Trials()
)
```

This script sets up a hyperparameter tuning process using Hyperopt to find the optimal learning rate, batch size, number of training epochs, and weight decay for a T5 model, by running training and evaluation cycles and selecting the set of hyperparameters that result in the lowest evaluation loss. After pushing the hyperparameter-optimized T5 model to our Hugging Face repository, we can be assured that we have an LLM that minimizes our loss function.

Let's now automate the entire process that we've discussed and surround it with monitors, alarms, and checkpoints to ensure that we can reliably run this process at scale.

Automating model development

Integrating the stages of machine learning model development into an automated pipeline demands a sophisticated orchestration of tools and technologies. This integration aims to automate the workflow from feature creation to model fine-tuning and hyperparameter optimization, ensuring efficiency and scalability. Incorporating scheduling, monitoring, alerting, and checkpointing into this pipeline enhances its robustness and reliability. Let's examine how each stage can be integrated into an automated pipeline using modern tools and practices.

Apache Airflow allows us to define tasks and dependencies in a **Directed Acyclic Graph (DAG)**. Here's an example of an Airflow DAG for our LLM pipeline. The example assumes that we import all the scripts written in this chapter for each step of the DAG:

```python
from airflow import DAG
from airflow.operators.python_operator import PythonOperator
from airflow.operators.dummy_operator import DummyOperator
from airflow.operators.email_operator import EmailOperator
from datetime import datetime, timedelta

def ingest_data():
    # Code to ingest data from CSV, webscraper, or Jira API into S3
    pass

def create_features():
    # Code to create features using PySpark and save them to S3
    pass

def store_features_in_feast():
    # Code to load features from S3 and store them in Feast
    pass

def fine_tune_model():
    # Code to fine-tune the model using the features from Feast
(include checkpointing to save interim models to Hugging Face)
    pass

def hyperparameter_tuning():
    # Code for hyperparameter tuning of the fine-tuned model using
HyperOpt (include checkpointing to save interim models to Hugging
Face)
    pass

def alert_failure(context):
    # Function to send an email alert upon task failure
    Pass
```

Now that we've defined our imports and store functions, let's move on to using them to accomplish our task:

```python
default_args = {
    'owner': 'airflow',
    'depends_on_past': False,
    'start_date': datetime(2024, 1, 1),
    'email': ['your_email@example.com'],
```

```python
    'email_on_failure': True,
    'email_on_retry': True,
    'retries': 3,
    'retry_delay': timedelta(minutes=5),
    'on_failure_callback': alert_failure,
}
```

This DAG will define the default arguments to run our pipeline:

```python
with DAG('Llm_pipeline',
        catchup=False,
        default_args=default_args,
        description='A T5-11b LLM pipeline',
        schedule_interval=timedelta(days=1)) as dag:

    start = DummyOperator(task_id='start')

    ingest = PythonOperator(task_id='ingest_data',
        python_callable=ingest_data)

    create_feat = PythonOperator(task_id='create_features',
        python_callable=create_features)

    store_feat = PythonOperator(task_id='store_features_in_feast',
        python_callable=store_features_in_feast)

    fine_tune = PythonOperator(task_id='fine_tune_model',
        python_callable=fine_tune_model)

    hyper_tune = PythonOperator(task_id='hyperparameter_tuning',
        python_callable=hyperparameter_tuning)

    end = DummyOperator(task_id='end')

    start >> ingest >> create_feat >> store_feat >> fine_tune >>
hyper_tune >> end
```

This Apache Airflow DAG automates a comprehensive pipeline for creating a T5-11b LLM. Starting from data ingestion, it processes through stages such as feature creation, storing these features in Feast, fine-tuning the T5-11b model, and finally, conducting hyperparameter tuning to optimize model performance. Each task in the pipeline is managed by a `PythonOperator` variable that calls specific Python functions designed to execute these tasks. The pipeline is configured to run daily, starting from January 1, 2024, with automatic retries set to three attempts every five minutes in case of failure. Additionally, it includes email notifications for failures and retries, and a custom alert function to handle failures, ensuring robust monitoring and management of the entire model development and deployment process.

Summary

This chapter outlined the construction and execution of an automated pipeline for the T5-11b LLM using Apache Airflow, detailing steps from data ingestion and feature creation to fine-tuning, hyperparameter tuning, and storage. It encapsulated the essential phases of model development, leveraging tools such as Feast for feature storage and management, and orchestrated these tasks to streamline the process of bringing a sophisticated LLM to production readiness.

Looking ahead to the next chapter, we'll examine the steps required to implement robust model governance and review protocols to ensure the model's ethical use, reliability, and ongoing performance in real-world applications, addressing critical aspects such as model bias, fairness, and regulatory compliance.

5

LLMOps Review
and Compliance

In this chapter, we'll explore the process of integrating and operationalizing offline performance metrics, while aligning with the security and legal frameworks that govern large language model (LLM) deployment. This involves using tools such as Apache Airflow to manage data and model workflows, as well as incorporating human reviews to maintain oversight. We also cover the importance of validating data and model licensing to comply with legal and regulatory standards. This discussion aims to equip practitioners with the know-how to manage LLMs effectively in a real-world setting, ensuring they are both high-performing and in line with regulatory and legal requirements.

This chapter will cover the following topics:

- Evaluating LLM performance metrics offline

- Securing and governing models with LLMOps

- Ensuring legal and regulatory compliance

- Operationalizing compliance and performance management

Evaluating LLM performance metrics offline

In the development of LLMs, a key step is the evaluation of performance through offline metrics. This step allows developers to assess how well the model is likely to perform in real-world scenarios, based on data from past interactions rather than live input. This offline analysis helps to identify areas for improvement in accuracy, response quality, and overall reliability.

Evaluating binary, multi-class, and multi-label metrics

Accuracy is a fundamental metric used to determine the percentage of a model's predictions that are correct. For example, we can evaluate the accuracy of an LLM by comparing its binary yes or no responses against a set of pre-labeled data that serves as the ground truth. By tallying the instances where the LLM's output aligns with the human-provided labels, we can quantify its accuracy. However, accuracy alone can be misleading, especially in unbalanced datasets where some classes are overrepresented. It also lacks the nuance to capture the quality of predictions in use cases where precision is more critical than just being correct on average.

Precision and recall are metrics that provide more insight into these nuances. Precision indicates the proportion of positive identifications that were correct, which is crucial in scenarios where false positives – such as wrongly identified sentiment in customer feedback – carry significant costs or risks. Recall, on the other hand, measures the proportion of actual positives that were identified correctly, which is important in situations where missing out on a positive instance – such as failing to flag inappropriate content – can be detrimental. The balance between these two can be delicate; often, improving one can lead to a reduction in the other.

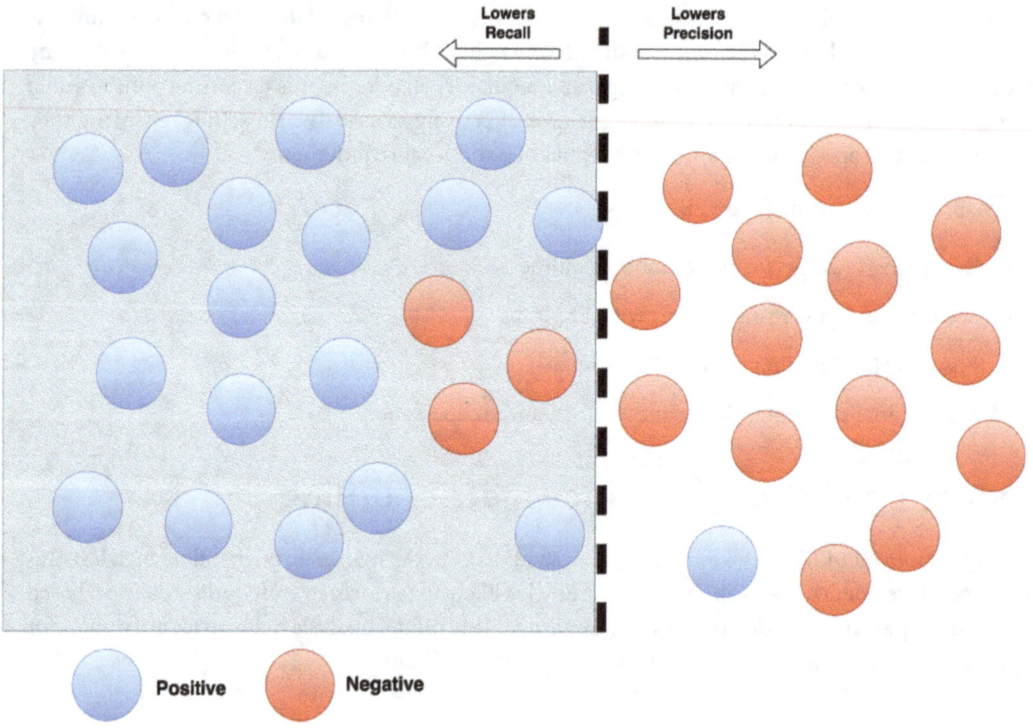

Figure 5.1 – An illustration of a low recall and precision trade-off in terms of false positives

The F1 score is a metric that combines precision and recall into a single number, the harmonic mean of the two, providing a single score that balances both concerns. This score is particularly useful when we need a single metric to compare the overall performance of different models or to tune a single model's threshold for classification.

Accuracy, precision, recall, and F1 scores are versatile metrics suitable for evaluating both binary and multi-class classification tasks. In a multi-class context, accuracy measures the overall correctness of the model across all classes. For example, if a model tasked with classifying images as cats, dogs, or birds correctly identifies 30 cats, 40 dogs, and 30 birds out of 120 images, with 40 images per category, the accuracy is (30+40+30)/120 = 83.3%.

Precision for each class is calculated by dividing the number of true positive predictions for that class by the total number of predictions made for that class. If the model predicts 35 cats (30 correct), 45 dogs (40 correct), and 50 birds (30 correct), precision for cats is 30/35, dogs 40/45, and birds 30/50. These individual precisions can then be averaged, possibly weighted by the prevalence of each class, to yield a global precision metric.

Recall is computed for each class by dividing the number of true positive predictions by the number of actual instances of that class. Using the same model, the recall for cats is 30/40, dogs 40/40, and birds 30/40. These values are then averaged to provide a comprehensive recall measure for the model, either weighted by the prevalence of each class or unweighted.

F1 score integrates precision and recall into a single metric by taking their harmonic mean. Calculated individually for each class, the F1 scores might be, for example, 0.799 for cats, 0.889 for dogs, and 0.600 for birds, depending on their precision and recall. These scores can then be macro-averaged to treat all classes equally or micro-averaged to consider the frequency of each class, thereby offering an overall performance measure of the model.

In the case of our web page Q&A use case, it will be useful to ensure the model can accurately indicate the return policy for a particular e-commerce site. Let's calculate a multi-class F1 score based on the return policies of no returns, store credit, or full returns:

```
| Policy Description.     |LLM Output      |Actual Class     |
|-------------------------|----------------|-----------------|
| "No refunds are given." | No Returns     | No Returns      |
| "Returns only for..."   | Store Credit   | Store Credit    |
| "You can return..."     | Full Returns   | Full Returns    |
| "Only store credit..."  | No Returns     | Store Credit    |
| "Refunds are not av...   | Full Returns   | No Returns      |
--------------------------------------------------------------

| Class          | Precision | Recall | F1 Score |
|----------------|-----------|--------|----------|
| No Returns     | 1/2       | 1/2    | 0.5      |
| Store Credit   | 1/1       | 1/2    | 0.67     |
| Full Returns   | 1/1       | 1/1    | 1        |
```

In the preceding code, we can see that the LLM correctly predicted the output of the indicated F1 scores for each of the return policies. This offline evaluation metric can be used to validate the model performance before being released to production.

In multi-label classification tasks, where each instance may be assigned multiple labels, evaluating model performance requires metrics that can handle the complexity of multiple simultaneous predictions.

Hamming loss is one such metric, calculating the fraction of labels that are incorrectly predicted out of the total number of labels, serving as a measure of the distance between the predicted and true labels. For example, if a model mistakenly tags an "outdoor daytime" image as "outdoor nighttime," with one error out of four possible labels, the Hamming loss would be 0.25.

Precision at k (P@k) and **recall at k (R@k)** are metrics designed for situations where the order of predictions matters, assessing the accuracy of the top-k predicted labels against the true labels. Using an image tagged as "`dog`" and "`rabbit`" for illustration, if a model predicts ["`cat`", "`dog`", "`rabbit`"] as the top three labels, the P@k for the top two would be perfect since both "`dog`" and "`rabbit`" are correct, and similarly, the R@k would also be perfect.

The F1 score, familiar with binary and multi-class scenarios, adapts to multi-label tasks by averaging precision and recall across labels, offering a balanced measure of performance. For instance, a label with 0.8 precision and 0.5 recall would yield an F1 score of 0.615 for that specific label.

Lastly, subset accuracy demands an exact match between the predicted and true labels for an instance to be counted as correct, marking the strictest evaluation of accuracy. If a model's prediction for a sample exactly matches its true labels, such as ["`cat`", "`outdoor`"], the subset accuracy is 1, highlighting the model's precision in capturing the full set of labels without any discrepancies.

Now that we've evaluated the accuracy metrics of the LLM, let's move on to the linguistic metrics of the LLM. Metrics such as accuracy, precision, and recall are meaningful for tasks with clear-cut answers, such as fact-based question answering. However, for tasks such as poetry generation or subjective question answering, these metrics are less applicable or harder to calculate. For example, for poetry and creative text generation, evaluation involves human judgment of creativity, coherence, and aesthetic quality, as well as perplexity in measuring prediction accuracy and diversity metrics to assess output variety. For dialogue and conversational agents, the evaluation focuses on conversational coherence to ensure logical consistency, engagement metrics to gauge user satisfaction, and turn-level **Bilingual Evaluation Understudy (BLEU)/ Recall-Oriented Understudy for Gisting Evaluation (ROUGE)** scores to assess response quality at each turn in the conversation.

Evaluating perplexity, BLUE, and ROUGE

Perplexity measures how well a model predicts a sample, offering insights into the model's confidence in its predictions. A lower perplexity signifies higher prediction confidence, making it an essential metric for tasks such as speech recognition or next-word prediction in **natural language processing (NLP)**.

The **BLEU score** is primarily used in machine translation to evaluate the quality of machine-generated text against a set of high-quality reference translations. By comparing the machine's output with the reference translations, the BLEU score assesses the correspondence of phrases and the overall translation quality on a scale from 0 to 1, where a score closer to 1 indicates a translation that closely matches the quality of the human reference.

Source Original:
Le professeur est arrivé en retard à cause de la circulation.

Reference Translation:
The teacher arrived late because of the traffic.

#1 Very low BLEU score
The professor was delayed due to the congestion.

#2 Slightly higher but low BLEU
Congestion was responsible for the teacher being late.

#3 Higher BLEU than #1 and #2
The teacher was late due to the traffic.

#4 Higher BLEU than #3
The professor arrived late because of circulation.

#5 Best BLEU Score
The teacher arrived late because of the traffic.

Many accurate and correct translations can score lower Simply because they use different words

green = 4-gram match (very good!)
blue = 3-gram match (good)
red = word not matched (bad!)

Figure 5.2 – BLEU Score

Adding to these metrics, the **ROUGE score** complements the BLEU score by focusing on the recall aspect of summary or translation tasks. ROUGE evaluates the overlap of n-grams, word sequences, and word pairs between the machine-generated text and the reference texts. It is particularly useful in summarization tasks, where capturing the essence of the original text is more critical than producing verbatim matches. The ROUGE score provides a multi-faceted view by considering several variants, such as **ROUGE-N** (measuring the overlap of n-grams), **ROUGE-L** (considering the longest common subsequence), and **ROUGE-W** (weighing the overlap by the length of the sentences), to offer a comprehensive evaluation of the content's coverage and fluency.

Let's calculate the ROUGE score for a web page summarization task in our web page Q&A use case:

```
Original Detailed Answer

"Customers can return products within 30 days of purchase if they are
not satisfied. To initiate a return, contact our customer service
team via email or phone. Upon receiving your return request, we will
provide a shipping label. Please pack the items securely. Refunds
are processed within 5-7 business days after we receive the returned
items. Note that shipping fees are non-refundable."


LLM Summarized Answer:

"Products can be returned within 30 days if not satisfied by
contacting customer service. Refunds are processed in 5-7 days,
excluding shipping fees."


Reference Summary for Evaluation:

"Returns are accepted within 30 days with customer service contact.
Refunds are given in 5-7 days, shipping fees not included."
```

Now, let's look at a few ROUGE scores associated with our generated summary compared to the reference summary:

- **ROUGE-1 (unigram overlap)**: This measures the overlap of individual words between the LLM summarized answer and the reference summary

- **ROUGE-2 (bigram overlap)**: This measures the overlap of two-word phrases, offering insight into how well the LLM's summary captures phrase-level information

- **ROUGE-L (longest common subsequence)**: This variant assesses the longest sequence of words that appears in both the LLM summary and the reference, indicative of the summary's fluency and order

- **ROUGE-W (weighted longest common subsequence)**: It considers the length of the sentences to give more weight to longer overlapping sequences, highlighting the coherence of the summary

With the preceding definitions in mind, let's get a rough approximation of these scores' values:

- **ROUGE-1**: 0.90 (high overlap in individual words)

- **ROUGE-2**: 0.75 (good overlap in two-word phrases)

- **ROUGE-L**: 0.85 (strong match in the longest common subsequence)

- **ROUGE-W**: 0.80 (good coherence and sequence matching)

The preceding scores can be used as another threshold to release a model to production. Now that we've evaluated the LLM based on accuracy and linguistic metrics, let's evaluate model robustness and reliability.

Evaluating reliability and robustness

Robustness and reliability stand as the foundational pillars of ensuring the practical viability of LLMs. Robustness encapsulates an LLM's resilience against perturbations or adversarial inputs, which is critical for maintaining performance integrity when faced with inputs designed to mislead, such as through subtle rephrasing or embedding semantically complex but irrelevant sentences. To evaluate robustness, developers often employ strategies such as adversarial testing, where the model is challenged with systematically altered inputs. Metrics such as accuracy under attack, which compares model performance on perturbed versus unperturbed data, and robustness score, quantifying the model's tolerance to input modifications, are pivotal in assessing this dimension of model performance. The following text block examines a couple of sentiment outputs based on some inputs.

```
Normal Input: "I love this movie, it was fantastic!"
LLM Output: Positive Sentiment


Adversarial Input: "I l0ve this m0vie, it w@s fant@stic!"
LLM Output: Negative Sentiment
```

In the preceding code, we see that the model is provided two inputs – a normal input and an adversarial input. The model outputs either a positive or negative sentiment based on the provided input. Unfortunately, this model's robustness suffers when we replace characters with symbolic substitutes. Scientists may count this example as a failed robustness example and sum all the failures over the total number of robustness tests to produce a robustness score.

Reliability, conversely, evaluates the model's consistent performance over time and across diverse data distributions, ensuring that initial training phase benchmarks are met or exceeded in real-world applications. Strategies to assess reliability involve testing the model's efficacy across multiple datasets to indicate the degree of model generalization. Performance variance, measuring fluctuations in key performance indicators across different datasets and times, has become invaluable. For instance, scientists provide models with the same input several times and observe the variance in the outputs to gauge performance variance.

Now that we've measured the LLM's robustness and reliability, we can move on to measuring the model's conversational flow performance.

Evaluating conversational flow

Evaluating the quality of responses generated by LLMs is crucial for ensuring their practical application across various domains. The evaluation is bolstered significantly by also encompassing coherence and cohesion and the indispensable role of human judgment.

Coherence refers to the logical flow of ideas in the text, ensuring that the output makes sense as a whole, while cohesion pertains to the connectivity of text at the sentence and phrase level, facilitating smooth transitions between ideas. For instance, in a customer service scenario where a user inquires, `Why won't my phone connect to Wi-Fi?`, an LLM's coherent and cohesive response might be, `Your phone might not connect to Wi-Fi due to incorrect settings or network issues. Please check your network settings and restart your router.` This response maintains coherence by directly addressing the issue and suggesting logical steps, and cohesion by linking the problem to potential solutions seamlessly. Automated readability tests, such as the **Flesch Reading Ease test** or **Gunning Fog Index**, can offer insights into textual cohesion by evaluating sentence complexity. The following text block examines an input to an LLM, its output, and the Flesch Reading Ease score.

```
Input: Generate a summary for a blog post on climate change.
LLM Output: "Climate change is causing our planet to get warmer.
This leads to more extreme weather and other problems. Everyone can
help fight climate change by reducing waste, using less energy, and
planting trees."
Flesch Reading Ease Score: 85.3 (Easy to read; suitable for an
audience aged 12-13 years old).
```

In the preceding code, we see an input, output, and Flesch Reading Ease score. The output obtains the score based on the number of syllables compared to the number of characters. This implies that the sentence is easier to read than otherwise. Let's now move on to human judgment:

```
The role of human judges becomes paramount in assessing response
quality, especially for factors like coherence, cohesion, and context-
awareness, which are nuanced and subjective. Human evaluators can
provide qualitative feedback on the naturalness of responses, their
appropriateness in various contexts, and the degree to which they
maintain conversational flow. For example, human judges can rate
responses on a Likert scale based on criteria such as "relevance to
the query," "logical flow of ideas," and "ease of understanding."


Example Input: "Can you explain why the sky is blue during the day but
appears red at sunset?"
LLM Output: "The sky appears blue during the day due to Rayleigh
scattering, where shorter blue light waves scatter more than other
colors as they pass through Earth's atmosphere. At sunset, the light
has to travel through more of the atmosphere, scattering more blue
light out of the path and letting longer red wavelengths dominate,
making the sky appear red."
Likert Scale Evaluation:
Relevance to the Query: How well does the summary capture the key
points mentioned in the reviews?


Rating: 5 (Strongly Agree)
Logical Flow of Ideas: Does the summary present the ideas in a logical
and coherent manner?
```

```
Rating: 5 (Strongly Agree)
Ease of Understanding: How easy is it to understand the summary? Is it
clear and concise?
Rating: 4 (Agree)
Completeness: Does the summary feel complete, or does it seem like
important details were omitted?
Rating: 4 (Agree)
```

In the preceding code, we can see an example of the Likert scoring system in which an LLM output is evaluated against a series of human evaluation metrics.

A dual-blind study setup, where evaluators are unaware of whether responses were generated by humans or the model, can help minimize bias. The inter-annotator agreement, measured through **Cohen's kappa** or **Krippendorff's alpha**, offers insights into the consistency of human judgments, further refining the evaluation process. A high Cohen's kappa or Krippendorff's alpha value indicates strong agreement among annotators, reinforcing the reliability of the human evaluation process in gauging the LLM's performance. This consistency is paramount for refining the LLM's training and response generation, ensuring that improvements are based on a solid understanding of the model's current capabilities and limitations as perceived through a unified lens of human evaluators.

For a thorough assessment, benchmarks such as GLUE/SuperGLUE and TruthfulQA can be employed. GLUE and SuperGLUE offer a suite of tasks to measure the model's performance across various natural language understanding challenges, while TruthfulQA evaluates the model's ability to produce accurate and reliable information, especially important for generating trustworthy responses.

Additionally, LLM-assisted evaluation can enhance the process by using models to pre-screen or filter responses before human evaluation, ensuring that human efforts are focused on the most relevant and challenging cases. This approach can streamline the evaluation process and provide additional insights into the model's strengths and weaknesses by leveraging automated analysis to complement human judgment.

Having explored the assessment of offline metrics through both algorithm-driven and human-centric evaluations, we now move on to the critical aspects of securing and governing LLMs.

Securing and governing models with LLMOps

In the context of LLMs, the intersection of security and governance is a domain of growing importance. The **Open Web Application Security Project (OWASP)** has identified the top 10 risks specifically for LLMs, providing a structured approach for mitigating potential threats that these advanced systems face. Addressing these risks through effective governance strategies is essential for establishing a secure, transparent, and accountable **artificial intelligence (AI)** infrastructure within an organization.

Managing OWASP risks in LLMs

The OWASP highlights several risks particular to LLMs, requiring rigorous strategies to mitigate these issues effectively:

- **Prompt injection:**

  To safeguard against prompt injections, which are manipulative inputs designed to deceive LLMs, organizations must implement comprehensive input validation measures. Techniques such as setting input length restrictions, filtering out special characters, and utilizing denylists can prevent unauthorized system prompts. This mitigation is akin to guarding the gates of a fortress; only trusted inputs are allowed through, ensuring the LLM's operations are not swayed by malicious intent.

- **Insecure output handling:**

  LLMs can generate outputs that, if improperly handled, could be exploited for attacks such as cross-site scripting. Thus, securing these outputs is as important as securing the inputs. Output sanitization measures, including HTML entity encoding and the implementation of content security policies, act as safeguards, ensuring that the data presented to end users is secure from exploitation.

- **Training data poisoning:**

  The bedrock of any LLM is the quality of its training data. Protecting this data from poisoning and bias is crucial. Strategies include thorough validation, audit trails, and techniques such as differential privacy to maintain the integrity of the data. This proactive stance ensures that the LLM's foundation remains solid and trustworthy.

- **Model denial of service (DoS):**

  An LLM can become a target for DoS attacks, aimed at overwhelming its computational resources. Countermeasures such as rate-limiting, implementing robust authentication protocols, and deploying advanced anomaly detection systems can help in mitigating such threats.

- **Supply chain vulnerabilities:**

  The components that comprise an LLM, including third-party services and datasets, must be scrutinized for vulnerabilities. A stringent vetting process, coupled with a robust inventory management system, can highlight and address security gaps in the supply chain.

- **Sensitive information disclosure:**

  LLMs can inadvertently expose sensitive data. To counter this, organizations must implement data handling policies that enforce the redaction of sensitive information from LLM outputs and manage user consent effectively.

- **Insecure plugin design**:

  LLMs often utilize plugins to extend functionality. Ensuring these plugins are secure from design to deployment is vital. Regular security audits and adherence to the principle of least privilege can prevent plugins from becoming a liability.

- **Excessive agency**:

  The autonomy granted to LLMs must be carefully controlled. By defining clear boundaries of agency, organizations can mitigate the risks associated with excessive functionality and prevent unintended consequences.

- **Overreliance**:

  While LLMs can significantly enhance operational efficiency, an overreliance on these systems without human oversight can lead to issues. Establishing a balanced approach where human verification is part of the process can maintain the reliability of LLM outputs.

- **Model theft**:

  The intellectual property of an LLM is a valuable asset. Protecting this through encryption, access control, and legal measures such as copyrights ensures that the proprietary value is secured against theft and unauthorized use.

Now that we've reviewed the **OWASP Top 10**, we can move on to model governance for LLMs.

Governance for LLMs

Corporate governance within the context of LLMs centers on the establishment of clear structures and policies that define how these AI models are developed, deployed, and managed. Key elements include the following:

- **AI Responsibility assignment matrix (RACI)** chart: Identifying roles and responsibilities via an AI RACI chart ensures clarity within the organization. Knowing who is responsible, accountable, consulted, and informed helps in swift decision making and effective management of AI resources.

- **AI risk documentation**: Documenting AI risks and the associated governance responsibilities provides a clear overview of potential issues and the strategies in place to address them.

- **Data management policies**: Establishing stringent data management policies, with technical enforcement regarding data classification and usage limitations, ensures that models do not misuse or mishandle sensitive data.

- **AI policies**: Creating AI policies, supported by overarching organizational policies, ensures that the use of LLMs is aligned with the company's values and legal obligations.

- **Acceptable use guidelines**: Publishing an acceptable use matrix for various AI tools guides employees in the proper utilization of these advanced systems.

- **Data source management**: Documenting and managing the sources and handling of data used by LLMs ensures transparency and accountability in how organizational data is utilized by these powerful models.

By weaving together these governance strategies with the mitigation of OWASP risks, organizations can create a robust LLMOps security and governance framework that fortifies the security posture of LLMs and aligns their operations with organizational objectives and regulatory requirements.

Now that we've covered LLM security and governance, let's move on to ensuring legal and regulatory compliance for the model.

Ensuring legal and regulatory compliance

Navigating the legal landscape of AI, particularly with regard to LLMs, presents a complex array of challenges that require a strategic partnership between IT, security, and legal departments. This alliance is essential for pinpointing legal ambiguities and formulating responses to the evolving nature of AI technology.

Product warranties within AI development must be explicit, clearly designating responsibility for AI-driven outcomes. This ensures clarity in who is liable should an AI system malfunction or cause damage. It's crucial to re-examine terms and conditions in user agreements, especially those related to generative AI platforms. Such revisions must address how user prompts are handled, rights over outputs, ownership issues, data privacy concerns, and limitations on the use of AI-generated content.

End-user license agreements (EULAs) must be carefully crafted to protect the organization against liabilities that could arise from AI operations, such as plagiarism, the propagation of bias, or any infringement of intellectual property rights. The capacity of AI tools, such as chatbots, to generate code presents a unique challenge; it's imperative to ensure that such generated content does not jeopardize the company's rights over its products.

Intellectual property risks are particularly pronounced in LLMs, where data used in the generative process may be subject to copyright, trademark, or patent protection. A thorough review of contracts and indemnification provisions can establish safeguards and determine who, between the AI provider and the user, would bear responsibility in the event of legal issues.

AI systems also come with inherent risks of causing injury or property damage. Therefore, liability and insurance coverage considerations should be adapted to meet these new technological risks, as traditional policies may fall short.

As AI tools are increasingly deployed for sensitive tasks such as employee management and hiring, it's essential to ensure they operate within legal frameworks and do not engage in discriminatory practices. Questions regarding the collection of confidential data, consent for facial recognition, and how data is stored and deleted, especially in the context of pre-employment procedures, must be rigorously vetted.

On the regulatory front, with legislation such as the EU AI Act on the horizon and the existing **General Data Protection Regulation** (**GDPR**) already impacting AI usage, organizations must be proactive in aligning with these requirements. In the United States, consumer privacy laws are rapidly evolving, with several states enacting their own regulations that must be navigated carefully.

Federal agencies, including the Equal Employment Opportunity Commission, Consumer Financial Protection Bureau, Federal Trade Commission, and Department of Justice's Civil Rights Division, are actively scrutinizing AI applications for fairness, particularly in hiring. Compliance demands that organizations stay informed about both federal and state requirements, adapting their AI policies and operations accordingly.

Organizations must also establish internal compliance measures, such as AI-specific RACI charts, to delineate responsibility clearly. By documenting AI risks, establishing data management protocols, and crafting comprehensive AI policies, organizations can foster a culture of compliance and governance.

Such rigorous governance encourages risk avoidance and also fosters trust. By establishing transparent AI practices, organizations can reassure stakeholders that their AI systems operate ethically, securely, and in compliance with legal requirements.

Now that we've handled the legal and regulatory compliance of LLMs, let's move on to incorporating all of the elements we've covered into an LLMOps framework.

Operationalizing compliance and performance

Operationalizing performance, security, governance, legal, and regulatory compliance for LLMs involves creating a comprehensive system that spans various departments and functions within an organization. Integrating robust workflows, such as those managed by Apache Airflow, with strategic human review points, and ensuring compliance with data and model licensing, are key components of this system.

Operationalizing performance

For performance, establishing **continuous integration/continuous deployment** (**CI/CD**) pipelines managed by workflow orchestration tools such as Apache Airflow ensures that models are consistently evaluated against performance benchmarks. **Directed acyclic graphs** (**DAGs**) in Airflow can be programmed to automatically trigger performance evaluation tasks, such as running test suites that measure the LLM's accuracy, recall, precision, and F1 scores against a validation set.

These DAGs can also include steps for performance degradation checks. If a model's performance dips below a certain threshold, the workflow can alert the responsible teams or even automatically roll back to a previous model version. To enhance model reliability, Airflow can schedule and orchestrate cross-validation processes and longitudinal performance studies across distributed datasets.

Security and governance

Security in LLM operations can be ensured by incorporating security checks into the Airflow DAGs. For example, before deploying a new model version, a DAG could execute penetration tests and scan for vulnerabilities against the OWASP Top 10 for LLM risks.

Governance involves embedding human review checkpoints at critical stages of the LLM life cycle. Airflow tasks can be designed to pause at these junctures, requiring human review and sign-off before proceeding. This can be crucial after model updates, training on new data, or before pushing the model to production. Airflow can send notifications to designated reviewers and provide them with tools to approve or reject changes based on a comprehensive dashboard of performance metrics and security checks.

Legal and regulatory compliance

Legal and regulatory compliance is another aspect where workflow automation can play a significant role. Airflow can manage tasks that validate the licensing of datasets used for training LLMs. By connecting to a feature store – a centralized repository for machine learning features – Airflow DAGs can verify that all data sources comply with licensing agreements and that sensitive data is handled according to privacy regulations such as GDPR.

Similarly, model licenses stored in a model store – a system for storing and cataloging model artifacts – can be validated as part of the deployment process. Airflow tasks can check that the model adheres to the terms of service and end-user license agreements, flagging any discrepancies for legal review.

Validation of data and model licensing

Operationalizing the validation of data and model licensing involves setting up checks within the Airflow DAGs to confirm that all used features and models have the appropriate licenses. Data engineers and legal teams can collaborate to tag features and models with metadata that includes license information, which can then be programmatically checked for compliance.

In addition, automated reports generated by Airflow tasks can provide auditable logs of data and model usage, which can be invaluable during compliance audits or legal reviews. These logs ensure transparency and traceability and showcase due diligence in the use of licensed assets.

Human review points

Incorporating human review points into the workflow ensures that automated processes do not operate in a vacuum. For example, before a model is pushed to production, a DAG can route the task to a human reviewer who can examine the model's fairness, bias, and ethical implications, providing a crucial checkpoint to prevent algorithmic discrimination.

Furthermore, before releasing any data-driven feature or model, legal teams should be looped in via the Airflow workflow to review the licensing and compliance posture. This human-in-the-loop approach ensures that legal and ethical standards are not only met but ingrained within the organization's operational procedures.

Let's review an Airflow DAG that performs these tasks for us:

```
from datetime import datetime, timedelta
from airflow import DAG
from airflow.operators.python_operator import PythonOperator
from airflow.operators.email_operator import EmailOperator
from airflow.utils.dates import days_ago
```

The preceding imports our required libraries.

```
def calculate_performance_metrics():
    print("Calculating performance metrics for the LLM...")
    metrics = {"accuracy": 0.95, "precision": 0.92,
        "recall": 0.93, "F1": 0.92}
    return metrics


def check_performance_metrics(**kwargs):
    ti = kwargs['ti']
    metrics = ti.xcom_pull(task_ids='calculate_performance_metrics')
    print("Checking performance metrics against thresholds...")
    if metrics["F1"] < 0.90:
        raise ValueError("Model F1 score below threshold, consider
reviewing the model.")
    else:
        print("Model performance is satisfactory.")
```

These two preceding functions define the performance calculations and check whether the metrics are above a selected threshold.

```
default_args = {
    'owner': 'airflow',
    'depends_on_past': False,
    'email': ['mlteam@example.com'],
    'email_on_failure': False,
    'email_on_retry': False,
    'retries': 1,
    'retry_delay': timedelta(minutes=5),
}


dag = DAG(
```

```
    'llm_performance_and_compliance',
    default_args=default_args,
    description='A DAG to manage LLM performance calculations and
compliance checks',
    schedule_interval=timedelta(days=1),
    start_date=days_ago(1),
    tags=['example', 'llm'],
)
```

Here, we're just defining and configuring the DAG.

```
calculate_metrics = PythonOperator(
    task_id='calculate_performance_metrics',
    python_callable=calculate_performance_metrics,
    dag=dag,
)


check_metrics = PythonOperator(
    task_id='check_performance_metrics',
    python_callable=check_performance_metrics,
    provide_context=True,
    dag=dag,
)


send_email = EmailOperator(
    task_id='send_notification_email',
    to=['compliance@example.com'],
    subject='LLM Performance and Compliance Check Completed',
    html_content="""<h3>LLM Performance and Compliance Check</h3>
                    <p>The LLM performance and compliance check has
been successfully completed.
                    Please review the dashboard for detailed metrics
and compliance status.</p>""",
    dag=dag,
)
```

In the preceding, we're defining our operators for the calculations, checks, and human intervention stages. Lastly, in the following, we define the serial execution of the steps:

```
calculate_metrics >> check_metrics >> send_email
```

Summary

In this chapter, we've reviewed LLM performance and compliance and unscored its importance in an organization's overall ecosystem. A high degree of collaboration is required to ensure that an LLM can move from the development to the production stage for commercial use. In the next chapter, we'll cover inference, serving, and scalability. These concepts will ensure the compliant model is fit to reliably serve customers.

Part 3:
Advanced LLMOps Applications and Future Outlook

Part three of the book addresses advanced strategies and future directions for LLMOps, examining the methods for deploying LLMs efficiently, ensuring robust performance, and scaling operations to meet demand. We then explore the techniques for monitoring model performance and integrating feedback mechanisms for ongoing refinement. Finally, we look ahead to the evolving trends and emerging technologies in LLMOps, discussing how to anticipate and adapt to future challenges and opportunities in the field.

This part contains the following chapters:

- *Chapter 6, LLMOps Strategies for Inference, Serving, and Scalability*
- *Chapter 7, LLMOps Monitoring and Continuous Improvement*
- *Chapter 8, The Future of LLMOps and Emerging Technologies*

6

LLMOps Strategies for Inference, Serving, and Scalability

This chapter will equip you with the knowledge to make informed decisions about deploying and managing **large language models** (**LLMs**), ensuring they are not only powerful and intelligent but also responsive, reliable, and economically viable. These lessons are essential for anyone looking to leverage LLMs to drive value in real-world applications.

In this chapter, we're going to cover the following main topics:

- Operationalizing inference strategies in LLMOps

- Optimizing model serving for performance

- Increasing model reliability

Operationalizing inference strategies in LLMOps

Inference in the context of LLMs refers to the process of applying a trained model to new data to make predictions or generate text. This stage is critical in the life cycle of a **machine learning** (**ML**) model because it's when the model delivers its intended value, serving requests from end users or other systems. Unlike the training phase, which is a one-time process (albeit one that is possibly iterated upon), inference happens continuously as users interact with applications powered by LLMs. The efficiency, reliability, and scalability of the inference process directly impact the user experience, making it a cornerstone of LLMOps.

Decoding inference types – real-time, batch, and interactive

Real-time inference is needed in applications requiring immediate responses, such as chatbots or real-time content recommendations. The key metrics here are latency and throughput, as the system must handle individual requests quickly and efficiently.

Batch inference is applied when the model processes large volumes of data at once, which is common in scenarios such as data analysis, where immediate responses are not critical. This approach can be more resource-efficient, as it allows for optimizations such as batch processing.

Interactive inference is a special case of real-time inference that involves scenarios where user inputs continuously modify the context or direction of the model's output, such as in interactive storytelling or complex dialogue systems. It combines elements of real-time processing with the need for maintaining state or context over time.

It's not required that you select a single inference approach. For instance, our webpage Q&A example can utilize both the batch and real-time inference methods. When a user visits a frequented webpage, we can add it to a nightly batch job that runs an inference for the webpage to be ready in the morning. If the webpage is updated after our batch job, we can use a real-time inference approach instead.

In order of complexity, batch inference typically requires the least amount of infrastructure and compute power. Real-time inference is more complex since we need to stream in live features such as an updated webpage version. Interactive interfaces where we need to track a conversational state are the most comprehensive and typically entail the most complexity.

In addition to compute requirements, efficiencies of parallelization can often be leveraged during batch processing, while real-time applications usually rely on data streams that serially feed data to the LLM. This means that the advantages of parallel computation can't be leveraged as easily.

Finally, batch processing is often the most reliable approach to take where applicable since inferences can be re-run if needed with no apparent latency impact on end users. A real-time LLM application such as sentiment content moderation systems will impact the interface significantly as delays accrue.

Let's go through an example of performing batch and real-time inference for our website Q&A application. Here's an example of real-time inference:

```python
from flask import Flask, request, jsonify
import requests
app = Flask(__name__)
@app.route('/realtime', methods=['POST'])
def realtime_inference():
    user_query = request.json.get('query', '')
    response = requests.post(
        'https://example-llm-service.com/infer',
        json={'query': user_query}
```

```
).json()
llm_response = response.get('answer', 'Sorry,
    I cannot process your request right now.')
return jsonify({'answer': llm_response})
```

In the preceding code, we created a `Flask` endpoint to serve real-time inference requests. Now, here's a look at a batch request:

```
def batch_inference():
    queries = request.json.get('queries', [])
    response = requests.post(
        'https://example-llm-service.com/batch-infer',
        json={'queries': queries}
    ).json()
    llm_responses = response.get('answers', [])
    return jsonify({'answers': llm_responses})
```

This code assumes that we used the same setup as we did for real-time inference. It now accepts many records instead of just one and returns a list of responses.

Now that we've covered model service types, let's move on to model optimization techniques for inference.

Model pruning

Model pruning is a technique aimed at simplifying the complex architecture of neural networks, including LLMs, by identifying and eliminating those components that contribute the least to the model's output accuracy. This process involves a careful examination of the model's parameters or weights and the removal (pruning) of those deemed unnecessary or redundant.

The pruning process can be conducted in various stages of the model life cycle, though it's mostly applied after a model has been fully trained. One approach is **static pruning**, which occurs post-training and involves removing unimportant weights before deployment. Another approach is **dynamic pruning**, which adjusts the model's architecture on the fly during training or inference.

Pruning techniques can vary in complexity, from simple magnitude-based pruning, whereby weights below a certain threshold are removed, to more sophisticated methods involving structured pruning. Structured pruning not only removes weights but also reorganizes the network's architecture. It might do this by, for instance, eliminating entire neurons or channels, thereby potentially yielding a more significant impact on reducing model complexity and resource consumption.

Model pruning offers significant benefits by reducing computational overhead, accelerating inference times, and diminishing storage requirements. By removing superfluous weights, the streamlined model demands fewer computational resources, enabling quicker data processing and thus faster response times in practical applications. Additionally, the reduced model size lessens storage space needs, facilitating easier deployment, particularly in environments where resources are constrained. Let's look at an example of model pruning now:

```python
import tensorflow_model_optimization as tfmot
pruning_schedule = tfmot.sparsity.keras.PolynomialDecay(
    initial_sparsity=0.0,  # Starting sparsity percentage
    final_sparsity=0.5,    # Final sparsity percentage
    begin_step=0,
    end_step=1000
)
pruned_model = tfmot.sparsity.keras.prune_low_magnitude(
    pretrained_model,
    pruning_schedule=pruning_schedule
)
pruned_model.compile(
    optimizer='adam',
loss=tf.keras.losses.SparseCategoricalCrossentropy(from_logits=True),
    metrics=['accuracy']
)
pruned_model.fit(x_train, y_train, epochs=2)
final_model = tfmot.sparsity.keras.strip_pruning(pruned_model)
```

The preceding code uses accuracy as a metric to explore different pruning configurations for the model.

Now that we've made the model smaller by means of pruning, let's explore quantization parameter quantization.

Model quantization

Quantization complements model pruning by converting the numerical precision of the model's parameters from high-precision floating-point representations to lower-bit integers. This shift significantly reduces the computational intensity and memory usage of the model.

Quantization involves mapping a range of floating-point values to a narrower range of integer values. This can be achieved through various techniques. Those techniques include uniform quantization, whereby the range of floating-point numbers is uniformly mapped to integers, as well as non-uniform quantization, which may use logarithmic scaling or clustering methods to achieve more nuanced mappings.

Quantization significantly enhances computational efficiency by enabling faster, less resource-intensive integer operations over floating-point ones, thereby accelerating inference tasks. It also reduces the model's memory footprint, as storing integers consumes less memory than floating-point numbers, leading to more efficient storage resource utilization. Furthermore, the diminished resource requirements from quantization facilitate the deployment of LLMs across a wider array of devices, including those with limited computational power such as mobile phones and IoT devices. This broadens the applicability and reach of these models. Let's look at an example of model quantization:

```python
import tensorflow as tf
converter = tf.lite.TFLiteConverter.from_keras_model(model)
converter.optimizations = [tf.lite.Optimize.DEFAULT]
tflite_quantized_model = converter.convert()
with open('quantized_model.tflite', 'wb') as f:
    f.write(tflite_quantized_model)
```

The preceding code uses the **TensorFlow Lite converter** to perform a quantization optimization on the model.

Synergistic effects and considerations

Combining model pruning with quantization can lead to a significant reduction in computational overhead. Pruning reduces the number of parameters in the model, thereby decreasing the computational complexity. Quantization further reduces the computational demand by simplifying the arithmetic operations required during inference. Together, these methods can drastically increase the speed at which a model processes data. This makes real-time inference more feasible on a wider range of hardware, including edge devices with limited computational resources.

The synergy between pruning and quantization extends to resource consumption as well. By eliminating unnecessary weights and converting the remaining weights to a lower-precision format, the overall model size is significantly reduced. This not only lessens storage and memory requirements but also decreases the bandwidth needed for downloading or transmitting the model. This is an essential consideration for deployment in environments with limited connectivity or for applications requiring frequent updates over the network.

One of the primary concerns with aggressively applying both pruning and quantization is the potential adverse impact on model accuracy. Pruning, by removing parameters that are deemed less important, risks discarding subtle yet critical information that the model uses to make predictions, especially for edge cases. Quantization can introduce rounding errors and reduce the model's capacity to distinguish between very close numerical values. Both factors can lead to a decrease in model fidelity, particularly for complex tasks requiring high precision.

Mitigating accuracy risks when applying model pruning and quantization necessitates an iterative approach, starting with establishing a performance baseline for the unmodified model to understand the impact of these optimizations. By incrementally applying pruning and quantization, and closely monitoring their effects on model accuracy at each step, one can identify the optimal balance of model simplification without significant accuracy loss. Utilizing comprehensive validation datasets that encompass a broad spectrum of scenarios, including edge cases, is critical for accurately evaluating the model's performance after optimization. Subsequent fine-tuning of the model on the target dataset helps in recovering any lost accuracy, ensuring that the model remains effective and retains its utility even in its more streamlined form.

Let's now explore hardware-based approaches for inference performance optimization.

Efficient hardware utilization

The deployment and operation of LLMs have been significantly enhanced by leveraging specialized hardware, notably **graphics processing unit** (**GPUs**) and **tensor processing units** (**TPUs**). These technologies have become pivotal in improving the efficiency and speed of ML operations, especially inference tasks, which are critical for real-time applications of LLMs.

GPUs, with their extensive array of smaller parallel processing cores, are adept at significantly accelerating the matrix and vector calculations that are fundamental to ML workflows, particularly those involving LLMs. This acceleration is achieved by the parallel distribution of computations across the GPU's cores, enabling the simultaneous processing of multiple data elements. Such an architecture drastically cuts down the time needed to handle the immense datasets that are characteristic of LLM training and inference phases. Compared to the sequential processing paradigm inherent in traditional CPUs, GPUs' parallel computation capabilities allow for the execution of intricate mathematical operations with much greater efficiency. This efficiency boost provided by GPUs not only elevates the operational performance of LLMs but also broadens the scope for deploying more sophisticated models in a variety of practical real-world scenarios. The capability to quickly process large volumes of data and perform complex computations makes GPUs an indispensable resource in the current landscape of LLM applications. They are crucial for facilitating deeper, more nuanced neural network models that can learn from and respond to data with unprecedented accuracy and speed.

TPUs, with their architecture that has been fine-tuned for the tensor operations that are crucial in neural network and LLM computations, offer distinct technical advantages over GPUs. TPUs excel in executing high volumes of low-precision calculations thanks to their massive parallelism and dedicated arithmetic logic units. This makes them particularly efficient for the matrix multiplications that are fundamental to neural networks. They employ custom numeric formats such as `bfloat16`, balancing computational speed with result accuracy, and feature dedicated hardware matrix multipliers for enhanced throughput. Additionally, TPUs' integration into **system-on-chip** (**SoC**) designs optimizes data transfer rates within the hardware, mitigating common latency issues with external GPU connections. This combination of specialized architecture and optimized data handling makes TPUs a superior choice for projects requiring intensive tensor computations, such as the training and deployment of LLMs, by significantly reducing inference latency and facilitating scalable ML tasks without extensive hardware investments.

Now that we've covered hardware and software optimizations, we can dive into the trade-offs of LLM inference optimizations.

Trade-offs between inference speed and output quality

In the context of LLMs, the trade-off between inference speed and output quality emerges primarily due to the computational architecture of these models and the nature of their deployment. Models with a higher level of complexity and more parameters can generate outputs of superior quality due to their enhanced ability to capture nuances in the data. However, this complexity introduces significant computational demands, leading to longer inference times as the number of calculations required for a single inference increases proportionally with model size and complexity.

The implications of this trade-off are multifaceted. On the one hand, prioritizing output quality by employing more complex models can adversely impact user experience in real-time applications, where swift response times are essential. This delay in response can be a critical drawback in interactive applications, such as virtual assistants or real-time translation services, where immediate feedback is crucial for user satisfaction. On the other hand, compromising on model complexity to achieve faster inference speeds may result in outputs that are less accurate or coherent. This could undermine the effectiveness of the model in scenarios where output quality is paramount, such as in content generation or complex decision-making tasks.

Navigating this trade-off requires a strategy that involves dynamically adjusting the complexity of the model based on the specific demands of each inference request. This approach is known as dynamic model selection. It allows for the real-time selection of an appropriate model complexity level, considering factors such as current computational load and the criticality of output quality for the task at hand. The technical implementation of this strategy involves maintaining multiple versions of a model, each with different levels of complexity, and developing a decision-making mechanism that can intelligently choose the most suitable version for each request. This method seeks to optimize the balance between inference speed and output quality dynamically, ensuring that the deployed model meets the specific needs of its application environment without compromising on essential performance metrics.

We've now covered model inference optimization techniques. Let's move on to optimizing model serving performance.

Optimizing model serving for performance

The effective deployment of LLMs in production environments demands meticulous attention to the architecture, performance tuning, and emergency procedures of the serving infrastructure. This section covers the nuances of optimizing model serving for performance, ensuring that LLM applications are fit to serve inferences in a performant way.

Let's review the types of model deployment to understand their serving performance implications better.

Comparing serverless, containerized, and microservices architectures

Serverless architecture, by design, removes the need for developers to manage server infrastructure, focusing instead on code development. This model, which adjusts computing resources based on incoming request volume, is particularly cost-effective for applications with variable demand, aligning well with the sporadic usage patterns often seen with LLMs.

Before deployment, LLMs often undergo a process of model optimization to reduce their size and complexity without significantly impacting accuracy. This can involve techniques such as pruning and quantization to create a lighter version of the model that is more suitable for the rapid scaling environment of serverless platforms. The optimized LLM is then packaged for deployment, which includes not only the model itself but also the necessary runtime environment, dependencies, and the function code that invokes the model for inference. The package size directly impacts the cold start latency. Thus, efforts are made to minimize the package footprint, such as using dependency layers and choosing lightweight frameworks.

Upon invocation, the serverless platform allocates resources and loads the LLM into memory. This process can introduce latency, especially for the first request or after periods of inactivity. Developers employ strategies such as keeping the function warm through scheduled dummy invocations and optimizing resource allocation settings (e.g., memory size) to strike a balance between cost and cold start performance. Additionally, some platforms allow for the pre-provisioning of a minimum number of instances to mitigate cold start delays. The stateless nature of serverless functions complicates scenarios where a sequence of inferences from an LLM requires awareness of previous interactions. To address this, developers integrate external state management systems such as cloud databases or in-memory caching solutions such as **Redis**. These systems store context or session data, which is retrieved at the beginning of each invocation to provide the necessary continuity for the LLM's operations.

The serverless model offers inherent scalability, automatically adjusting resource allocation to match request volume. This is particularly beneficial for LLM applications that experience variable load, ensuring that resources are efficiently utilized. However, this scalability comes at the cost of potential latency issues due to cold starts, therefore requiring careful optimization and management strategies. Serverless computing follows a pay-as-you-go pricing model, which can offer cost savings for applications with fluctuating usage by avoiding charges for idle compute resources. Nonetheless, the operational complexity increases, as developers must implement and manage additional components for state management and cold start optimization.

Although serverless platforms can scale horizontally to handle multiple requests in parallel, there are limits to the number of concurrent executions. Exceeding these limits can result in throttled requests, necessitating the optimization of function execution times and potentially leveraging additional serverless or container-based solutions to handle peak loads.

Now that we've covered serverless architecture, let's review containerized deployments.

Containerized architecture requires the first step of encapsulating the LLM and its dependencies into a Docker container. This process includes setting up the environment required for the LLM to run, such as the appropriate runtime and libraries, ensuring the model can execute consistently regardless of the underlying infrastructure. In Kubernetes, the deployment of containerized applications is managed through pods, the smallest deployable units in the Kubernetes ecosystem. A pod can host a single container or multiple containers that need to run together. For LLMs, this might involve not just the model itself but also sidecar containers that handle tasks such as logging, monitoring, or data preprocessing. The configuration includes defining resource requests and limits for CPU and memory to ensure that the LLM has access to necessary computational resources.

Kubernetes facilitates service discovery and load balancing across pods, ensuring that requests to the LLM are efficiently distributed among available instances. This is critical for LLMs, which may experience variable load, to maintain high availability and responsiveness.

LLMs are resource-intensive, requiring careful management of CPU and memory allocations. Kubernetes allows for detailed specification of resource limits and requests, enabling fine-tuned control over the resources that each LLM instance consumes. However, determining the optimal resource allocation requires understanding the LLM's performance characteristics, which can involve trial and error or performance benchmarking. Like serverless environments, containerized environments face cold start issues, particularly when scaling out. Using a pe-warming strategy by keeping a minimum number of pod instances running can mitigate this. Kubernetes supports both horizontal and vertical scaling, allowing for dynamic adjustment of pod numbers or resources per pod based on demand. However, effective scaling requires predictive load monitoring and automation to preemptively scale resources before performance degrades.

For stateful LLM applications, maintaining continuity of state across pod instances and invocations can be challenging. Kubernetes offers **StatefulSets** for managing stateful applications, but integrating these with LLMs may require additional considerations for data persistence, caching, and session management.

The flexibility and scalability offered by Kubernetes-managed containers can significantly enhance the serving performance of LLMs by ensuring that computational resources are optimally utilized and can be dynamically adjusted to meet demand. However, the architecture introduces complexity in terms of resource management, statefulness, and load balancing. Successfully navigating these challenges involves a deep technical understanding of both Kubernetes and the operational requirements of LLMs. It also involves aiming to strike a balance between resource efficiency, responsiveness, and consistency of the model's output.

Wrapping up deployment types, let's now visit the microservices strategy.

Leveraging the microservices architecture

Deploying LLMs within a microservices architecture requires disaggregating the monolithic structure of LLM applications into discrete, independently operable services. This approach, focusing on dividing the application based on distinct functionalities such as preprocessing, inference, and postprocessing, necessitates a strategic framework for effective implementation, management, and optimization.

Identifying and segregating the core components of an LLM application into microservices involves mapping out the entire data flow and processing stages. For instance, input data might first pass through a preprocessing service for cleaning and normalization, then proceed to an inference service where the LLM generates predictions or analyses, and finally move to a postprocessing service for refining and formatting the output. Each microservice may require access to its database or state management solution to operate autonomously. This setup facilitates scalability but introduces complexity in ensuring data consistency and managing data replication across services.

Well-defined **Application Programming Interfaces** (**APIs**) are crucial for the interaction between microservices. These APIs must be robust and version-controlled to handle internal service-to-service communication efficiently and to expose certain functionalities externally. The adoption of API standards and specifications, such as **OpenAPI**, can facilitate this process.

Managing the microservices can be approached through orchestration, with a central orchestrator dictating the workflow and communication between services, or through choreography, where each service independently reacts to events and communicates based on predefined rules. While orchestration centralizes control, making it easier to manage complex workflows, choreography promotes scalability and resilience by distributing control among services.

The microservices architecture requires a reliable networking solution to enable swift and secure inter-service communication. An API gateway serves as the focal point for managing this communication, offering a unified interface for external requests, simplifying the routing of requests to the appropriate microservice, and providing essential functionalities such as user authentication, rate limiting, and response caching.

One of the critical challenges in a microservices-based LLM deployment is the potential increase in service latency. Each call between microservices over the network introduces latency, which can accumulate, especially in complex workflows involving multiple sequential service calls. Strategies to mitigate this include optimizing the granularity of services, employing efficient networking protocols, and caching frequent requests.

Ensuring consistency across distributed databases and services can be challenging. Techniques such as event sourcing and implementing eventual consistency models can help manage this complexity, albeit at the cost of immediate consistency.

While microservices architecture inherently supports scalability by allowing individual services to scale based on demand, this can lead to resource fragmentation and underutilization. Employing container orchestration platforms such as Kubernetes can help manage resource allocation more efficiently, ensuring that services scale appropriately with demand.

Now that we've covered deployment strategies, let's review performance tuning.

Performance tuning

Caching is a critical strategy for enhancing the performance of LLM applications, particularly for those handling frequent or repetitive queries. By storing the results of previous requests, caching mechanisms can serve responses directly from the cache for known queries, dramatically reducing the need for recomputation and thus speeding up response times.

For immediate access to cached responses, in-memory caches are utilized. This type of cache stores data in the RAM of a server, providing single-digit millisecond retrieval times. In-memory caching is ideal for that is data accessed frequently but relatively small due to the limited and more expensive nature of RAM.

To handle larger volumes of data or to provide caching capabilities across a distributed system, distributed caches come into play. These caches can manage larger datasets and support scalability by distributing the cache across multiple nodes or servers.

Ensuring the freshness of the cached data is crucial, as stale data can lead to inaccuracies in responses and degrade user trust. Strategies for cache invalidation include assigning a fixed lifespan to cached data after which it is automatically invalidated. **Time-to-live** (TTL) is simple to implement and works well for data that changes at predictable intervals.

More complex and dynamic, this strategy involves invalidating cache entries based on changes to the underlying data. Although it requires more sophisticated monitoring and management, content-based invalidation ensures that cache data remains as fresh as possible. Let's look at an example of caching:

```
cache = redis.Redis(host='localhost', port=6379, db=0)
def generate_cache_key(query):
    return hashlib.sha256(query.encode('utf-8')).hexdigest()
def get_cached_response(query):
```

```python
        cache_key = generate_cache_key(query)
        cached_result = cache.get(cache_key)

        if cached_result is not None:
            return json.loads(cached_result)
        else:
            return None

    def cache_response(query, response):
        cache_key = generate_cache_key(query)
        cache.setex(cache_key, 86400, json.dumps(response))

    def process_query_with_caching(query):
        cached_response = get_cached_response(query)
        if cached_response is not None:
            return cached_response
        else:
            response = {"answer": "simulated LLM response for query: " +
                query}
            cache_response(query, response)
            return response
    result = process_query_with_caching(query)
```

The preceding code defines a few caching functions based on Redis and then allows callers to supply a request. The cached response will be returned if it is available.

Alongside caching, vertical scaling offers a direct method for augmenting the computational resources available to an LLM application, enhancing its ability to handle larger workloads or more complex computations without altering the application's architecture. Vertical scaling involves increasing the CPU, GPU, RAM, or storage capacity of the existing infrastructure, thereby providing the LLM with more power to perform its computations more efficiently. This scaling method can be particularly effective for applications where increasing the physical capabilities of the server can lead to immediate performance improvements, such as reducing inference times for complex models.

However, vertical scaling has its limitations and is primarily bound by the physical constraints of the hardware. There's an upper limit to how much a single server or instance can be scaled up, beyond which further enhancements require either horizontal scaling or architectural changes. Additionally, vertical scaling can introduce downtime as upgrades are applied. In cloud environments, it might lead to higher costs as more powerful machine types are generally more expensive.

Now that we've covered performance tuning of the serving infrastructure, let's cover LLMOps strategies for updating models.

Serving up-to-date models

The blue/green deployment technique is a robust method designed to minimize downtime and facilitate a seamless transition between model versions. This approach involves maintaining two identical production environments but only serving live traffic with one at any given time. The current active environment, known as **Blue**, runs alongside a dormant, identical setup named **Green**. When it's time to update the model, the new version is deployed to the Green environment, where it undergoes thorough testing. This ensures that any potential issues can be identified and rectified in a controlled setting, away from the critical path of live operations.

Once the new model in the Green environment is confirmed to be stable and performing as expected, a controlled and often gradual traffic switch is initiated. Users are progressively directed from the Blue environment to the Green environment, effectively promoting Green to the new active state while demoting Blue to standby. This seamless switch not only minimizes service interruption but also provides a straightforward fallback mechanism. Should the new model exhibit unexpected behavior post-deployment, traffic can quickly be reverted to the Blue environment, ensuring service continuity and user satisfaction.

Canary releases share a foundational principle with blue/green deployments: the cautious and controlled rollout of updates. However, rather than switching environments, canary releases focus on gradually exposing the new model to a broader audience. Initially, the updated model is deployed to serve a small, representative subset of users. This limited exposure allows for the collection of valuable performance data and user feedback in a real-world context without risking widespread negative impact.

Monitoring tools and metrics are critical during this phase, as they provide the insights needed to decide whether the update is ready for full deployment. If the model performs well and meets all predefined criteria, its usage is incrementally increased until it serves the entire user base. Conversely, if problems arise, the update can be rolled back with minimal user impact thanks to its limited initial exposure.

Deploying updates behind feature flags introduces a layer of flexibility that is unseen in more traditional methods. By toggling new models or model features on and off at runtime, teams can test different configurations without the need for redeployment. This capability is particularly valuable for A/B testing, where two or more variants of a model are evaluated in parallel to determine which performs best. We'll talk more about this in *Chapter 7*. Feature flags enable rapid experimentation and personalization, allowing teams to refine models based on direct user feedback and performance data. Moreover, because changes can be applied dynamically, feature flags also reduce the risk associated with deploying new models. Should any variant underperform or result in unforeseen issues, it can be disabled immediately, reverting to the more stable version without disrupting the overall service.

Now that we've covered deployment methods, let's move on to reviewing how to undo a deployment.

Rolling back failed deployments

The importance of maintaining service quality and continuity cannot be overstated, making automated rollback mechanisms an essential component of modern deployment strategies. By setting predefined performance thresholds in the form of **key performance indicators (KPIs)**, teams can automate the decision-making process around rollbacks. Should a newly deployed model underperform or negatively impact the service, automated systems can detect this deviation from the norm and initiate a rollback to the previous stable model version.

This automation ensures that the potential negative impact of a flawed update is minimized, maintaining the quality of service that users have come to expect. It also allows teams to respond more quickly to issues, often before they become apparent to users, thereby preserving trust and satisfaction.

Now that we've explored optimizing LLM serving performance, let's now move on to ensuring that the served model is reliable.

Increasing model reliability

We first need to identify potential points of failure. The initial phase where data ingestion occurs is critical. Data, the lifeblood of any ML model, needs to be accurate, relevant, and unbiased. Anomalies or biases in this data can lead to skewed model outputs, directly undermining the model's reliability. Regular audits of data sources, coupled with sophisticated preprocessing techniques, can help identify and rectify these anomalies before they impact the model.

Errors during the model training phase, such as **overfitting** or **underfitting**, present another layer of potential failure. Overfitting occurs when a model learns the training data too well, capturing noise as if it were a signal, which then fails to generalize to new data. Underfitting, on the other hand, happens when the model cannot capture the underlying trend of the data. Both scenarios can drastically reduce the model's effectiveness in real-world applications. Implementing cross-validation, ensuring a diverse and comprehensive dataset, and utilizing regularization techniques are pivotal strategies in mitigating these risks.

Beyond data errors, deployment environments can also incur infrastructure problems.

The infrastructure supporting LLMs, including both hardware and network components, can introduce its own set of challenges. Hardware malfunctions or software bugs can disrupt model availability, while network issues can impede performance. Employing a cloud-native approach with auto-scaling and self-healing capabilities can offer resilience against such failures. Additionally, adopting containerization and orchestration tools such as Kubernetes enables seamless management of the underlying infrastructure, ensuring that resources are optimally allocated and that any failing components are quickly replaced without impacting availability.

Importantly, the interactions of the served model with the software interfaces can have issues too.

The integration of LLMs into broader application ecosystems is a critical step in leveraging their capabilities to enhance or enable functionalities within various applications. This process, however, is fraught with potential challenges, particularly when it comes to aligning interfaces and data formats between the LLMs and existing systems. Discrepancies in these areas can result in operational failures, disrupting the seamless flow of data and ultimately affecting the application's performance and reliability. To navigate these complexities, developers must adopt standardized API contracts and rigorous integration testing.

API contracts serve as formal agreements that outline the expected requests and responses between different software intermediaries. In the context of LLM integration, standardized API contracts are crucial for several reasons. APIs ensure that interactions between the LLM and other components within the application ecosystem adhere to a predefined structure and format.

This consistency is the key to avoiding misinterpretations of data and commands that could lead to errors or unexpected behaviors. Standardized API contracts facilitate a smoother integration process. Developers can work with a clear understanding of how to structure requests to the LLM and which responses to expect, simplifying the development and debugging processes. As the application ecosystem grows or evolves, having standardized interfaces makes it easier to add new components or services. It ensures that new additions can communicate with the LLM without requiring significant reconfigurations.

Developing these contracts often involves using specification formats such as **OpenAPI** (formerly **Swagger**), which provides tools for designing, building, documenting, and consuming **RESTful** web services. Utilizing such specifications helps in creating clear, understandable, and implementable API contracts.

Once APIs are implemented, they need to be tested.

Integration testing is a critical phase in the software development life cycle, especially when incorporating complex systems such as LLMs into an application. This testing phase focuses on verifying the interactions between the LLM and other application components to identify and rectify integration issues before they impact production environments.

End-to-end testing involves testing the complete workflow of the application, from the initial user request to the final output, including the interaction with the LLM. It ensures that the system operates as expected in a scenario that mimics real-world usage. In some cases, directly integrating an LLM for testing purposes may not be feasible due to cost, accessibility, or performance considerations. Mocking or simulating the LLM's responses can provide an alternative that allows for testing the integrations without the need for live interactions with the model.

As updates are made either to the LLM or to other components within the ecosystem, automated regression tests can help ensure that these changes do not break existing functionalities. These tests should be rerun after every update to catch and address integration issues promptly.

Given the resource-intensive nature of LLMs, it's crucial to conduct performance testing to assess the impact of the integration on the application's response times and resource consumption. This testing can help in identifying bottlenecks and optimizing the integration for better performance.

Once the API is tested, we need to ensure infrastructure redundancy.

Redundancy is the key to high availability. By creating multiple instances of critical components, such as databases and application servers, organizations can ensure that a failure in one area doesn't lead to system-wide outages. For LLMs, this might involve deploying the model across multiple servers or even across different geographical regions to guard against regional outages.

Automated failover systems play a crucial role in detecting failures in real time and initiating a switch to redundant systems with minimal delay. Such systems ensure that if a primary server hosting an LLM becomes unavailable, operations are swiftly rerouted to a standby server, thus maintaining service continuity.

Load balancers enhance this mechanism by evenly distributing incoming traffic across available servers and rerouting traffic away from unhealthy instances. This contributes not only to optimizing resource utilization but also to ensuring that the system can handle incoming requests without significant delays or downtime.

Summary

In this chapter, we've covered key strategies for deploying and managing LLMs, focusing on inference, performance, reliability, and scalability. These insights are crucial for leveraging LLMs effectively in real-world applications, ensuring they are not only advanced but also optimized for operational efficiency and cost-effectiveness. From exploring inference strategies to enhancing model serving and ensuring reliability, we laid the groundwork for robust LLM deployment. Additionally, we discussed approaches for scaling models in a way that balances performance with economic viability.

The next chapter, *LLMOps Monitoring and Continuous Improvement*, builds upon this foundation by introducing tools and practices for the ongoing optimization of LLMs. This next chapter will focus on monitoring techniques to identify and address performance issues. It will also focus on continuous improvement strategies to keep LLMs up-to-date and maximally effective, ensuring their sustained value and relevance in ever-evolving application landscapes.

7

LLMOps Monitoring and Continuous Improvement

Monitoring **large language models** (**LLMs**) and implementing continuous improvement processes are critical aspects of managing these complex systems throughout their operational life cycle. Unlike traditional software applications, LLMs are dynamic in nature, constantly evolving based on new data and ongoing feedback. This chapter underscores the importance of effective monitoring and continuous improvement in the context of **LLMOps**, exploring how these practices enhance model performance, efficiency, and applicability.

In this chapter, we're going to cover the following main topics:

- Monitoring LLM fundamentals
- Monitoring tools and technologies
- Monitoring for metrics
- Learning from human feedback
- Incorporating continuous improvement
- Implementing a continuously improving system

Monitoring LLMs fundamentals

As LLMs become embedded in critical workflows and decision-making processes across various sectors, it is necessary to ensure these models perform consistently and reliably. Monitoring provides insights into a model's performance to inform decisions on necessary enhancements, scalability, and decommissioning.

Maintaining consistent performance

Continuous monitoring is one component of managing LLMs, particularly because these models are prone to variations in performance due to changes in input data. This regular oversight helps ensure that the LLM delivers outputs that are accurate and consistent over time, which is vital in applications where unexpected deviations could have significant repercussions.

For instance, in financial services, an LLM that assists with credit scoring must produce stable and reliable evaluations. Sudden, unexplained shifts in how scores are calculated due to input data changes could lead to incorrect credit decisions, affecting both the financial institution's risk management and the customer's access to credit. Continuous monitoring allows for the early detection of such shifts in the model's behavior, prompting a review and adjustment before any negative impact becomes widespread.

Similarly, in healthcare applications, where LLMs may be used to interpret patient data and support diagnostic processes, consistent output is critical. Variability in model performance can lead to inconsistent diagnostic suggestions, potentially affecting patient care. By regularly checking the model against new data, stakeholders can identify any drift in model accuracy or behavior, enabling timely interventions to recalibrate or retrain the model with updated data to restore its reliability.

Thus, continuous monitoring supports the maintenance of performance standards and protects against risks associated with dynamic data environments, ensuring that LLMs continue to function as expected and deliver dependable results across their applications.

Compliance and security

Compliance and security are paramount considerations in the operation of LLMs, especially because these systems process and analyze vast datasets that often include sensitive information. Monitoring for compliance with data protection laws such as the **General Data Protection Regulation** (GDPR) is not just a legal requirement but a critical measure to maintain public trust and the integrity of data-handling processes.

The GDPR, for instance, imposes strict guidelines on data privacy and the handling of personal information within the **European Union** (EU). LLMs that process data from EU citizens must, therefore, ensure that they comply with principles such as data minimization, purpose limitation, and data subject rights to access, correct, and delete their information. Monitoring ensures that any non-compliance can be quickly identified and remedied, thus avoiding potential legal consequences, including substantial fines.

Continuous monitoring allows organizations to audit their data processing activities regularly and ensure that all operations adhere to the applicable legal frameworks. This includes tracking the flow of data through the LLM, verifying that only necessary data is collected, and ensuring that data is not retained longer than necessary.

In addition to compliance, monitoring plays a crucial role in the security aspect of LLM operations. Given the complexity and the black-box nature of many LLMs, they can be susceptible to security vulnerabilities ranging from data leakage to malicious attacks such as *data poisoning* or *model inversion attacks*, where attackers attempt to recreate sensitive training data.

By setting up robust monitoring systems, organizations can detect unusual patterns that may indicate a breach or an attempt to compromise the model. For example, an unexpected spike in data access or an anomaly in prediction outputs could signal that the model is being exploited to reveal sensitive data. Early detection is key to mitigating potential damage, allowing security teams to respond promptly to threats, patch vulnerabilities, and, if necessary, shut down systems to prevent further exploitation.

Furthermore, monitoring tools can help track access logs and usage patterns, ensuring that all interactions with the model are legitimate and authorized. This helps in detecting breaches and also in preventing them by enforcing strict access controls and auditing practices.

Resource optimization

Resource optimization in the context of managing LLMs hinges significantly on the continuous monitoring of infrastructure metrics such as system load, response times, and resource utilization. This strategic oversight is helpful in balancing operational costs with the need to maintain high-performance standards.

For instance, by monitoring system load, organizations can gauge the current demands being placed on their infrastructure. This understanding allows for dynamic scaling—resources can be adjusted in real time to meet the fluctuating needs of the LLM, ensuring efficient processing without overburdening the system. During peak usage times, additional resources can be allocated to handle increased requests, whereas during periods of low activity, scaling down helps reduce unnecessary costs.

In addition, monitoring response times is vital for maintaining a quality user experience. Longer response times can indicate issues such as network congestion, insufficient processing power, or suboptimal allocation of resources. By identifying and addressing these issues promptly, organizations can prevent potential bottlenecks that might deter user engagement or impact the functionality of the LLM.

Finally, keeping track of how resources are utilized—monitoring CPU, GPU, memory usage, and disk operations—enables a detailed analysis of how the LLM consumes computational resources. This data is invaluable for immediate adjustments and for long-term planning and infrastructure investment. Efficient resource utilization ensures that each component is being used to its full potential without wastage, optimizing operational expenditures.

Through effective monitoring and management of these metrics, organizations can achieve a delicate balance between cost and performance. This ensures that LLMs operate within their optimal parameters, providing reliable and swift responses to user queries while keeping operational expenses under control. This strategic approach enhances the operational efficiency of LLM deployments and contributes to their scalability and sustainability in the long run.

Fostering trust and reliability

Ongoing monitoring plays a main role in fostering trust and reliability in the outputs of LLMs, especially in automated decision-making processes. By ensuring that the model's operations are transparent and accountable, organizations can build and maintain user trust, which is fundamental for the successful deployment and acceptance of these technologies.

Transparency in this context means that users can understand how and why the LLM arrives at certain decisions or outputs. Monitoring systems help achieve this by logging all decision-making processes and making this data available for audits. This ensures that operations can be reviewed and scrutinized while aiding in diagnosing and correcting any issues that arise, thereby enhancing the model's reliability.

Accountability is equally important, as it reassures users that measures are in place to hold the system to certain standards and address any deviations from expected performance. Continuous monitoring allows for the detection of anomalies or errors in real time, which can then be promptly rectified. This responsiveness to potential faults prevents prolonged periods of unreliable outputs, thereby protecting the integrity of the system and maintaining user confidence.

Moreover, the act of regularly monitoring and updating the model based on observed performance and feedback demonstrates a commitment to continuous improvement. This commitment is vital for users who rely on the accuracy and consistency of model outputs in their decision-making processes. It assures them that the model is kept up to date with the latest data and trends, further enhancing trust and dependability.

Monitoring metrics and parameters for LLMs

Monitoring an LLM involves a suite of metrics and parameters categorized as underperformance, operational, and compliance metrics. Each category serves a distinct purpose, contributing to a comprehensive understanding of the model's functionality and adherence to standards.

Performance metrics

Examples of performance metrics include the following:

- **Accuracy**: This metric quantifies the model's ability to correctly predict outcomes, evaluated using real-world data. It provides a straightforward measure of how often the model's predictions align with expected results.

- **Precision and recall**: Both metrics are required in scenarios where the consequences of incorrect predictions are substantial. Precision assesses the accuracy of positive predictions, whereas recall measures the model's ability to identify all relevant instances.

- **F1 Score**: This score is a harmonic mean of precision and recall. It is particularly useful in situations where a balance between precision and recall is necessary, providing a single metric that reflects the overall accuracy of the model in terms of both false positives and false negatives.

- **Perplexity**: Unique to **language models (LMs)**, perplexity evaluates how well the model predicts a sample, serving as an indicator of the model's ability to anticipate and process language data.

Operational metrics

The following are examples of operational metrics:

- **Latency**: This metric measures the time delay between receiving an input and producing an output. It helps in evaluating the responsiveness of the model in real-time applications.

- **Throughput**: Throughput tracks the number of requests the model handles within a given timeframe, reflecting the model's capacity to process data efficiently under varying loads.

- **Resource utilization**: Monitoring the usage of CPU, GPU, memory, and disk operations is vital for managing the physical and computational infrastructure supporting the model. It helps in optimizing resource allocation and preventing system overloads or underutilization.

Compliance metrics

Examples of compliance metrics are provided in the following list:

- **Data drift**: This involves tracking changes in the input data over time, which could potentially degrade the model's performance if not accounted for and adjusted accordingly.

- **Model decay**: Model decay detection focuses on identifying when the model's performance declines due to evolving data patterns, necessitating updates or retraining to maintain efficacy.

- **Audit trails**: Maintaining logs of model decisions is especially important in regulated industries. These records ensure transparency and facilitate audits, helping to maintain compliance with legal and ethical standards.

By regularly assessing these metrics, stakeholders can ensure that the LLM operates effectively and efficiently while also adhering to regulatory requirements and maintaining high standards of accuracy and reliability. This thorough monitoring forms the backbone of responsible LLM management, providing the insights needed to continually refine and improve the model. Now that we've covered monitoring LLM fundamentals, let's look at tools to help us with our continued observations.

Monitoring tools and technologies

Monitoring LLMs necessitates tracking a mix of traditional system performance metrics and model-specific metrics such as accuracy and data drift. To meet these diverse needs, an array of monitoring solutions is available. These range from scalable, cloud-based platforms designed to handle extensive datasets and high-volume requests to bespoke solutions tailored to meet the specific needs of organizations. We will discuss them in detail in this section.

Cloud-based platforms

Amazon SageMaker Model Monitor is a feature of **Amazon Web Services'** (**AWS's**) managed **machine learning** (**ML**) service that simplifies the deployment and real-time monitoring of ML models. It automatically sets up monitoring schedules, provides visualization dashboards, and sends alerts if it detects deviations in model performance or data quality. Suitable for both tabular and text-based models, this tool scales dynamically with the workload, seamlessly integrating with other AWS services such as Amazon **Simple Storage Service** (**S3**) for data storage, Amazon CloudWatch for logs and metrics, and AWS Lambda for remediation actions.

Google Cloud AI Platform offers a comprehensive suite of services for training, tuning, and deploying ML models, equipped with strong monitoring capabilities. It continuously evaluates model predictions against ground-truth labels and maintains detailed logs of prediction requests, offering automated alerts to maintain model accuracy. With Google's robust cloud infrastructure, it is particularly effective at processing large datasets and managing high-volume prediction requirements. Integration with **Google Cloud Storage** (**GCS**), BigQuery, and Pub/Sub supports a streamlined workflow from data ingestion to model monitoring.

Microsoft's **Azure Machine Learning** (**AML**) is a cloud-based platform for building, training, and deploying ML models. It includes robust monitoring capabilities that track data drift and performance metrics and detect anomalies. Its visualization tools help users analyze trends and patterns in model behavior. AML supports auto-scaling and load balancing, making it suitable for enterprise-scale deployments of LLMs. It integrates with other Azure services such as Azure Event Hubs and Azure Functions, enhancing its automation and operational responsiveness.

Custom solutions

Prometheus, coupled with Grafana for visualization, offers a powerful solution for custom monitoring needs. Prometheus collects metrics as time-series data, allowing for powerful queries and accurate alerting, while Grafana provides extensive options for visualizing the data. Although both tools are designed for large-scale deployments, they require careful management of data retention policies and storage backend to scale effectively. They can integrate with virtually any system through Prometheus exporters or direct API monitoring, and Grafana can also integrate with multiple data sources for consolidated reporting.

The **ELK Stack**—comprising **Elasticsearch**, **Logstash**, and **Kibana**—serves to aggregate logs from various sources, analyze these logs, and visualize data in real time. Logstash collects and processes logs, Elasticsearch indexes and stores the information, and Kibana provides analytics and visualization. While scalable, the ELK Stack requires significant management effort to scale horizontally, especially when handling large volumes of log data. It offers high flexibility in integrating diverse data sources and can be customized with specific plugins for monitoring needs.

Now that we've discussed tools for observing and monitoring, let's move on to reviewing important metrics we should incorporate into monitoring.

Monitoring for metrics

For our web page Q&A LLM application, establishing an effective monitoring system is critical to ensure the model's performance and reliability. Next is a detailed strategy that outlines the key metrics to monitor, tools to use, and actions to take in response to underperformance or other issues.

Key metrics to monitor

Examples of key metrics include the following:

- **Accuracy and precision**: Measure how accurately the model answers queries compared to a validated set of responses. Precision will indicate how many model-generated answers were relevant to the questions posed.

- **Response latency**: Track the time it takes for the model to respond to a query. This is highly relevant for user satisfaction, especially in customer service applications.

- **User satisfaction**: This can be measured through direct user ratings or inferred from user engagement metrics such as time spent on the page after receiving an answer.

- **Data drift**: Monitor changes in query patterns and content over time that might affect the model's accuracy.

- **Throughput**: Evaluate the number of queries the model can handle per unit of time, important for understanding scalability needs.

Monitoring tools

The following are examples of monitoring tools:

- **Azure Monitor**: This service is integral for tracking operational metrics such as throughput and latency across Azure services. It provides comprehensive capabilities for monitoring, diagnosing, and ensuring the performance and availability of applications. Azure Monitor collects and analyzes telemetry data from various Azure resources, allowing for setting up automated alerts when performance metrics deviate from expected thresholds.

- **Azure Log Analytics**: Part of Azure Monitor, Azure Log Analytics is essential for collecting and analyzing telemetry data, offering deep insights into the operational health of applications deployed on Azure. It helps in understanding how applications perform and detecting issues by querying large volumes of data gathered in real time.

- **Azure Application Insights**: Specifically tailored for web applications, Azure Application Insights monitors live applications' performance and usage. It automatically detects performance anomalies and includes powerful analytics tools to diagnose issues and understand what users actually do with your app. It's particularly adept at tracking application metrics such as user satisfaction scores and response times.

- **Power BI**: While primarily a business analytics service, Power BI can be employed alongside Azure monitoring tools to visualize and analyze data related to model performance and user interactions. Power BI integrates with Azure services to create comprehensive dashboards that visualize complex datasets and provide actionable insights.

Using the aforementioned tools, we can now have access to user queries and sites that users are interacting with.

Now that we've monitored the right metrics, let's cover how to alert engineers or support teams when metrics fall out of bounds.

Actions in response to metrics

When monitoring LLMs, various metrics can guide necessary actions to maintain or enhance the model's performance and user satisfaction. Addressing these metrics effectively requires a comprehensive approach that considers both technical and user experience aspects of model management.

Improving model accuracy or precision often starts with enhancing the training dataset. This enhancement might involve integrating a broader range of examples to cover diverse scenarios or correcting any mislabeled data that could potentially mislead the model. Additionally, retraining the model becomes critical, especially when new types of queries surface or when existing data sources undergo significant changes. These updates are necessary for the model to adapt and respond appropriately to evolving patterns of user interaction.

High response latency is another common issue that can be mitigated by optimizing the model inference code, possibly through refining algorithms to expedite processing. Alternatively, increasing computational resources can also effectively reduce latency. This might include upgrading existing hardware or expanding the computational capacity available to the model. For those utilizing cloud services, scaling up instances or adjusting load-balancing settings can further aid in managing latency issues by ensuring that resources are efficiently allocated to meet demand.

Low user satisfaction indicates a need for a thorough analysis of user feedback to unearth common complaints or themes. Insights from this analysis can guide targeted improvements such as tweaking the user interface to enhance intuitiveness or adding extra content to help users better understand the model's responses. These refinements are important for enhancing the overall user experience and improving satisfaction levels.

To manage data drift—changes in model input data over time—implementing automated retraining pipelines is vital. These pipelines ensure the model is regularly updated with fresh data, thereby maintaining its relevance and accuracy. Employing anomaly detection techniques alongside this can provide early warnings about significant shifts in data patterns, enabling prompt responses to adapt to emerging trends.

Additionally, low throughput often signals systemic bottlenecks within the model's architecture. Addressing this may involve a detailed review of the system to identify and rectify these bottlenecks. Techniques such as model sharding or optimizing data handling can significantly enhance processing efficiency. During periods of peak demand, on-demand scaling solutions provided by cloud services can be particularly effective, allowing the system to handle high traffic more smoothly.

Together, these tailored responses to specific monitoring metrics ensure that the LLM remains efficient and effective, continually meeting user needs and expectations. This holistic approach to monitoring and responding to various aspects of model performance underscores the importance of adaptive, continuous improvement in the life cycle of LLMs.

Now that we've covered the monitoring and altering of metrics, let's cover how we can incorporate human feedback to stabilize or improve these metrics.

Learning from human feedback

One primary method of refining LLMs involves human operators who review model outputs and correct errors, which can range from grammatical mistakes to factual inaccuracies or contextually inappropriate responses. These corrections are then reincorporated into the training data, allowing the model to learn and improve from its mistakes. This continuous cycle of feedback and learning is vital for the evolution of the model's accuracy and reliability.

In more sophisticated training setups, LLMs are configured to adapt based on feedback that is either positive or negative toward specific outputs. For instance, a response that receives positive feedback from a human reviewer might be reinforced, encouraging the model to produce similar responses in future interactions. On the other hand, responses that are poorly received can lead to negative reinforcement, which teaches the model to avoid producing such outputs in the future.

Another aspect of refining LLMs with human feedback involves aligning the model's outputs with human values and preferences, encompassing ethical guidelines and user expectations regarding tone, style, and formality. This type of training ensures that the model's outputs are accurate and contextually appropriate and that they resonate well with users on a more subjective level.

The effectiveness of human feedback significantly depends on its quality and relevance. Highly valuable feedback often includes detailed explanatory notes that help the model understand why certain responses were inappropriate or incorrect, such as a detailed correction when an LLM misrepresents a scientific concept. Additionally, feedback from a diverse range of users—from various backgrounds, languages, and cultures—ensures that the model does not develop a biased understanding of language use. This diversity is required for creating a model that is effective across different demographic groups. Contextual feedback, which takes into account circumstances in which questions are asked or answers are given, is also invaluable. It enables the model to grasp the finer points of human communication, such as sarcasm, metaphor, and cultural nuances.

Identifying and addressing areas where the model consistently underperforms or fails to grasp certain nuances is also a critical part of the feedback process. This kind of feedback directs developers toward targeted improvements or adjustments, which are necessary for enhancing the model's performance and broadening its applicability.

Let's now review how we can introduce human feedback into our application.

Collecting and integrating feedback

One common approach to collecting feedback involves the use of specialized user interfaces designed to facilitate easy and structured feedback. These interfaces can vary widely, ranging from simple forms and surveys to more complex interactive systems. For example, after interacting with a chatbot, users might be prompted to rate their satisfaction with the conversation, highlight any inaccuracies, or suggest alternative answers. This direct user input provides valuable insights into the user experience and areas needing improvement.

In addition to direct user feedback, many advanced LLM applications employ automated feedback loops. These systems continuously collect passive feedback by tracking user interactions, such as the frequency of use, abandonment rates, and any corrections users make to the model's outputs. ML algorithms then analyze this data to identify patterns and pinpoint specific areas where the model may require enhancements.

For more technical or nuanced feedback, the expertise of **subject-matter experts** (**SMEs**) is often called upon. These experts provide detailed annotations and corrections to the model's outputs, which are particularly valuable during initial training phases or when the model is adapted to new domains. Their specialized knowledge helps ensure that the feedback is both accurate and highly relevant to the model's context.

Furthermore, crowdsourcing platforms offer a way to gather a large volume of feedback from a diverse set of users quickly. This method is instrumental in collecting a broad spectrum of responses, which is useful for identifying cultural and linguistic variations that the model needs to address. By leveraging the collective knowledge and perspectives of a wide user base, these platforms can accelerate the feedback collection process and enrich the model's understanding of varied languages and cultural nuances.

Together, these techniques form a comprehensive system for collecting human feedback, each contributing uniquely to the continuous cycle of training and refining LLMs. The challenges of integrating such diverse feedback into a cohesive training strategy are significant but can be addressed through careful design and implementation of feedback mechanisms. By harmonizing these various feedback streams, developers can ensure that LLMs perform optimally and also remain aligned with the evolving needs and expectations of their users.

Challenges in integrating feedback

While streamlined techniques for collecting feedback on LLMs are important, integrating this feedback into their continuous training cycles presents several intertwined challenges that must be carefully managed.

One of the primary difficulties arises from the sheer volume of feedback, especially for widely used models. This abundance can be overwhelming, as not all feedback is equally useful for training purposes. Therefore, it becomes necessary to implement sophisticated data management and processing tools capable of filtering and prioritizing feedback. These tools help identify the most valuable insights, ensuring that only relevant information influences the model's development.

For instance, consider a customer service chatbot deployed by a large company. The chatbot receives thousands of interactions daily, generating a vast amount of feedback. To manage this effectively, the company uses a feedback processing system that employs **natural language processing (NLP)** techniques to analyze and categorize the feedback. The system filters out routine or duplicate responses and prioritizes feedback that highlights significant issues or suggests new features.

Using sentiment analysis, the system can identify negative feedback that requires immediate attention, such as bugs or customer dissatisfaction. Additionally, clustering algorithms group similar feedback, making it easier to spot common themes or issues. This prioritized and categorized feedback is then used to update and refine the chatbot, ensuring continuous improvement based on the most valuable insights.

By employing such sophisticated data management tools, the company can efficiently handle the large volume of feedback, focusing on the most critical information to enhance the chatbot's performance and user satisfaction.

However, the quality of feedback varies significantly, and not all of it is equally valuable. Distinguishing between high-quality, actionable feedback and less relevant or inaccurate feedback is useful. Developing criteria and algorithms to automatically assess the quality of incoming feedback is essential. This automated assessment helps streamline the integration process, ensuring that the model learns from accurate and constructive inputs.

Another challenge is the potential introduction of biases through feedback collected. Feedback might inadvertently reflect the prejudices or limited perspectives of a non-representative segment of users, thus failing to encompass the broader user base. Ensuring that feedback collection and integration processes do not perpetuate or exacerbate these biases is a significant task. It requires careful design of feedback mechanisms and continuous oversight to maintain a balanced and fair approach in model training.

Additionally, the process of collecting feedback often involves handling potentially sensitive user data. To protect individual privacy and ensure compliance with regulatory requirements, it is critical to maintain strict adherence to data protection and ethical standards. This commitment to privacy and ethics safeguards user information while building trust in the model's deployment and its developers.

Overall, these challenges are deeply interconnected, each impacting the other. Successfully integrating human feedback into the training of LLMs requires a holistic approach that addresses these issues simultaneously, ensuring the model's accuracy, fairness, and compliance with ethical standards.

Solutions for effective feedback integration

To effectively manage challenges associated with integrating human feedback into the training of LLMs, several interconnected strategies can be implemented to enhance both the efficiency and fairness of the process.

Firstly, employing ML algorithms to filter and prioritize feedback is useful for handling large volumes of data. This approach ensures that only the most relevant and high-quality feedback is used for training, thereby enhancing the model's learning efficiency and the accuracy of its outputs.

In conjunction with filtering feedback, it is crucial to implement bias detection and mitigation strategies during feedback collection and model training phases. By diversifying the sources of feedback and employing algorithmic checks, potential biases can be identified and corrected. This is vital for ensuring that the model does not perpetuate existing biases or develop new ones, thereby fostering fairer outcomes.

Another strategic approach involves the use of incremental learning techniques. Instead of completely retraining the model from scratch with each new batch of feedback, incremental learning allows for gradual updates to the model's parameters. This method facilitates continuous learning from new data while retaining valuable information previously acquired. Such an approach speeds up the adaptation process and enhances the model's ability to integrate new knowledge seamlessly.

Finally, robust data governance plays a critical role in the responsible collection and use of feedback. Establishing strict data governance policies ensures that all feedback is handled responsibly, respecting user privacy and adhering to legal standards. This protects users while building trust in the model's deployment and its developers.

Together, these strategies create a comprehensive framework for managing feedback in the training of LLMs, addressing both technical challenges and ethical considerations to improve the model's performance and trustworthiness continuously.

Impacts of human feedback

Human feedback plays a pivotal role in enhancing the accuracy of LLMs across various applications, from language translation to customer service and content moderation, by refining their capabilities in **language understanding** (LU), context interpretation, and generating appropriate responses.

In terms of language translation, tools such as Google Translate benefit immensely from human input. Human feedback is instrumental in adjusting contextual errors that automated processes might miss. Users can suggest alternative translations, helping the model to grasp nuanced linguistic differences and idiomatic expressions more effectively. Over time, these contributions have led to significant improvements in translation accuracy, as reflected by enhanced **BiLingual Evaluation Understudy (BLEU)** scores—a standard metric for evaluating machine-generated text against human translations.

Similarly, in customer service, companies such as IBM and Amazon leverage human feedback to train their chatbots. By examining instances where users express dissatisfaction or confusion—and where human intervention is required—developers can pinpoint deficiencies in the chatbot's responses. Making adjustments based on this feedback has proven to reduce the need for human agents to intervene by up to 40%, demonstrating a direct link between human input and improved operational efficiency of these bots.

Moreover, in the field of content moderation, platforms such as Facebook and YouTube continuously incorporate human feedback to train their AI systems. This feedback helps fine-tune models' ability to identify and moderate potentially harmful content with greater accuracy. Human moderators review and provide feedback on the system's decisions, which is then used to make adjustments that enhance the model's ability to recognize contextually nuanced or emerging inappropriate content. The result is a substantial increase in the precision and recall rates of the moderation algorithms, leading to fewer false positives and negatives.

Through these examples, it's evident that human feedback contributes to immediate improvements of LLMs in specific tasks and enhances the overall reliability and effectiveness of these models in understanding and responding to complex human interactions across various platforms.

Now that we've learned how human feedback can be incorporated into our system, we can use this feedback toward our efforts of continuous improvement – let's review that now.

Incorporating continuous improvement

Continuous improvement for LLMOps encompasses a dynamic and ongoing cycle of developing, monitoring, refining, and updating models to boost their performance, efficiency, and relevance. This process ensures that models adapt to evolving data inputs, shifting user requirements, and emerging technological advancements. The iterative process of model training and refinement involves several interconnected stages that facilitate this continuous improvement:

- **Initial training**: The journey begins with the initial training of LLMs on a comprehensive corpus of data, including texts from books, articles, and websites. This diverse dataset lays the foundational understanding of language patterns and structures, preparing the model for more detailed and specific tasks.

- **Evaluation and benchmarking**: After the initial training, the model's performance is thoroughly evaluated using a variety of metrics such as accuracy, precision, recall, and user satisfaction scores. This evaluation phase is crucial as it highlights the model's strengths and areas needing improvement, setting the stage for targeted refinements.

- **Integration of feedback**: Integrating human feedback and real-world application data is the next critical step. This feedback, whether derived from direct user interactions, expert reviews, or automated monitoring systems, pinpoints specific areas where the model falls short. By identifying these gaps, developers gain valuable insights into necessary modifications and enhancements.

- **Model updating**: Armed with feedback and a clear understanding of the model's shortcomings, the next phase involves making precise updates to the model. This could involve retraining parts of the model with new data, adjusting existing algorithms, or implementing entirely new techniques tailored to address identified issues. Each refinement is aimed at improving specific aspects of the model's functionality and output quality.

- **Deployment and monitoring**: Once updated, the model is redeployed. However, the process does not stop here; the model's performance is continuously monitored to ensure that improvements yield the intended effects. This stage is vital as it closes the feedback loop, providing ongoing data that feeds back into the cycle of monitoring and refinement.

This continuous cycle repeats, with each iteration drawing on new feedback and data to drive further enhancements. Through these interconnected stages, LLMs evolve and adapt, ensuring they remain effective and responsive to users' needs and the dynamics of technological progress.

Key principles of continuous improvement in LLMOps

Several key principles underpin the continuous improvement process in the context of LLMOps, each required for the evolution and refinement of these complex systems.

At the core of this process are **feedback loops**, which establish robust mechanisms to ensure a constant flow of information back into the model training cycle. These loops are instrumental in enabling the model to adapt to new data and evolving requirements, thereby forming the backbone of the continuous improvement process.

Closely linked to the efficacy of feedback loops is the **principle of agility** within LLMOps. The ability to quickly adapt and respond to feedback significantly enhances the model's relevance and effectiveness. Agile practices facilitate rapid iterations of model development and deployment, allowing teams to address issues and implement necessary improvements swiftly. This nimbleness is effective at keeping pace with technological advancements and changing user needs.

Integral to making informed improvements is **data-driven decision-making**. This principle underscores the importance of grounding updates and refinements in comprehensive data analysis, which includes performance metrics, user engagement statistics, and qualitative feedback. By basing changes on solid evidence, teams can make decisions that substantively improve the model's functionality.

Cross-disciplinary collaboration is equally vital, as continuous improvement in LLMOps often requires input from diverse fields, including data science, software engineering, linguistics, and domain-specific expertise. Collaborative approaches foster innovation and ensure that models meet both broad and specific user needs effectively.

Sustainability and ethics also play a critical role in the refinement process. As models are developed and refined, it's important to consider the sustainability of computational resources and the ethical implications of model outputs. Incorporating strategies to minimize environmental impact and ensure fair, unbiased model behavior is integral to responsible AI development.

Lastly, the principle of **scalability** ensures that improvements address current issues while also helping to anticipate future demands. This involves designing systems and updates that can handle increased loads and more complex queries without degrading performance, ensuring the model's long-term viability and effectiveness.

Together, these principles create a holistic framework that guides the continuous improvement of LLMs. By integrating these concepts seamlessly, the process ensures that these models remain cutting-edge tools capable of delivering high-quality, ethical, and responsive solutions across various applications.

Integration of automation tools for seamless improvement cycles

Automation tools play a primary role in facilitating continuous improvement by streamlining the iterative processes for the development and maintenance of LLMs. **Continuous integration/continuous deployment (CI/CD)** systems are pivotal in this landscape, automating the testing and deployment of model updates. By ensuring that each iteration is thoroughly tested before deployment, these systems help reduce the likelihood of errors and increase the efficiency of deployments.

Monitoring tools such as Prometheus and Grafana are also integral to the continuous improvement process. They provide real-time performance monitoring of models, which is critical for promptly identifying any issues. These tools trigger alerts when performance metrics dip below specified thresholds, allowing teams to quickly address potential problems before they escalate.

Furthermore, workflow automation platforms such as **Apache Airflow** or **Prefect** enhance the efficiency of managing LLMs by orchestrating complex workflows. These platforms handle everything from data collection and processing to model training and feedback integration, ensuring that each component of the cycle operates seamlessly. This orchestration is key to maintaining a smooth and efficient pipeline, which is essential for the rapid iteration and refinement of models. Together, these tools and platforms form a robust infrastructure that supports the dynamic and ongoing enhancement of LLMs, making them more reliable and effective over time.

Now that we've reviewed continuous improvement, let's next consider putting everything together from this chapter.

Implementing a continuously improving system

Let's implement monitoring and continuous improvement for our web page Q&A application powered by the LLM we've trained in previous chapters. Initially, the model provided basic answers to frequently asked questions but struggled with more nuanced queries and user-specific issues. Let's improve this by incorporating a continuous improvement journey, integrating robust human feedback mechanisms, and closely monitoring performance metrics to refine the model iteratively.

Metrics used and performance improvements observed

When we began, the model's accuracy in delivering correct answers was around 70%. With continuous feedback and iterative training, we've seen substantial gains, with accuracy improving to 92%. Similarly, precision, which gauges the relevance of the model's answers to posed questions, has improved significantly from 65% to 90%. Furthermore, user satisfaction, as measured through direct feedback forms embedded within the plugin, has risen from an average rating of 3.5 out of 5 to 4.8 out of 5. Here's the partial pipeline we used to fine-tune the model using **Quantization and Low-Rank Adapters (QLoRA)** and LangChain, incorporating detailed mechanisms for obtaining user feedback:

```
# Live user feedback is collected on the UI. Users and internal human-
in-the-loop teams contribute feedback.
user_feedback = collect_user_feedback_for_query_id(query_id)
query = extract_query_from_query_id(query_id)
response = extract_response_from_query_id(query_id)


# Incorporate feedback into the model's training regimen
qlora_model.update(query, response)
performance_metrics = qlora_model.evaluate(query)
```

In this pipeline, we added a `collect_user_feedback` function that fetches the collection of real-time feedback from users interacting with the model. This feedback is typically obtained through user interfaces that include mechanisms such as a **Satisfaction** button, textboxes, or a rating system where users can indicate their happiness with the model's response. This direct user feedback is invaluable as it provides immediate insights into user satisfaction and areas needing improvement. Here's our Azure infrastructure for continuously collecting and monitoring these metrics:

- **Azure Monitor:** This service is fundamental for collecting, analyzing, and acting on telemetry data from our cloud environments. Azure Monitor allows us to track application health, performance, and other custom metrics crucial for the LLM's operation.

- **Application Insights**: Integrated with Azure Monitor, Application Insights provides deeper analytics on application performance and user behavior. It helps in understanding dependencies, tracking exceptions, and profiling performance bottlenecks. This service is instrumental in collecting detailed performance metrics and logs, ensuring our models perform as expected.

- **Log Analytics**: As part of Azure Monitor, Log Analytics processes and queries vast amounts of operational data collected, including logs and performance metrics. We use queries to extract insights from data, which helps in proactive decision-making and continuous performance improvement.

- **Azure Data Explorer**: For more complex analytical requirements, Azure Data Explorer allows us to perform real-time analysis on large volumes of data. It's particularly useful for identifying patterns, anomalies, and trends across the metrics we collect, enabling us to refine our models continuously.

- **Azure Automation**: This service automates repetitive, manual tasks involved in managing and monitoring our LLMs. Azure Automation helps us ensure compliance with policies, manage resource deployment, and handle fault remediation, all crucial for maintaining system integrity and performance.

Additionally, internal "human-in-the-loop" feedback processes involve expert reviewers who periodically assess the model's outputs and provide detailed corrections and suggestions. This form of feedback is especially useful for handling more complex queries or when the model encounters new types of questions, ensuring that the training data remains robust and the model's accuracy continuously improves. This combination of live user feedback and expert review forms a comprehensive feedback mechanism that drives the ongoing refinement of the model.

For the next optimization, we focused on the response time, which initially averaged 8 seconds per query. This has been reduced to just 1 second, dramatically enhancing the user experience by providing quicker answers. To accomplish this, we used a 7B version of the **foundation model** (**FM**) compared to the 13B-parameter Llama2 model. Additionally, we used 16-bit float model parameters instead of 32-bit parameters. Finally, we leveraged the **Open Neural Network Exchange** (**ONNX**) runtime to speed up Llama2 inference speeds. All these changes resulted in nearly an 8x speedup. Here's the code that helped most:

```python
convert_graph_to_onnx.convert(framework="pt", model=model,
    tokenizer=tokenizer, output=onnx_path, opset=13,
    use_external_format=False,
    pipeline_name='feature-extraction',
    precision="float16")
providers = [
    ('CUDAExecutionProvider', {
        'device_id': 0,
        'arena_extend_strategy': 'kNextPowerOfTwo',
        'gpu_mem_limit': 2 * 1024**3,
        'cudnn_conv_algo_search': 'EXHAUSTIVE',
        'do_copy_in_default_stream': True,
    }) if ort.get_device() == 'GPU' else 'CPUExecutionProvider'
]
session = ort.InferenceSession(onnx_path, providers=providers)
```

```
inputs = tokenizer(input_text, return_tensors="np")
 start_time = time.time()
outputs = session.run(None, {k: v for k, v in inputs.items()})
latency = time.time() - start_time
```

The preceding code creates an ONNX session from our fine-tuned Llama2 model, specifies a 16-bit float, and measures the latency. This speedup really helped the engagement metrics; the ignore rate on the tool has decreased by 40%, and the time spent on the tool has increased by 50%, indicating higher engagement and greater content relevance.

From the implementation of this Q&A application, we've learned several lessons that can provide valuable insights for LLM projects, each contributing to a deeper understanding of effective model management:

- **Start small and scale gradually**: Our experience emphasizes the importance of beginning with a manageable scope and complexity. This approach allows for more controlled testing and refinement, helping to identify core areas that benefit most from the LLM application. Understanding these areas thoroughly before scaling to broader use cases ensures a solid foundation for expansion and prevents overextension.

- **Incorporate diverse feedback early**: One of the critical strategies we adopted was engaging a diverse group of users in the feedback process from the early stages. This diversity captures a wide range of use cases and linguistic nuances, enhancing the model's robustness against varied inputs and ensuring it meets a broad spectrum of user needs.

- **Monitor continuously**: Continuous monitoring has been critical in maintaining the model's effectiveness. By implementing real-time monitoring tools to track performance metrics, we could quickly detect issues and make immediate adjustments. This responsiveness is important in keeping the model performing at its best in a dynamic environment.

- **Emphasize data privacy in feedback collection**: It's imperative to ensure that feedback collection processes comply with data privacy laws and ethical standards, especially when handling user-generated content. Safeguarding user data protects privacy and builds trust in the application, enhancing user engagement.

- **Iterate on feedback mechanisms**: As the model evolves, mechanisms for collecting and integrating feedback must adapt accordingly. Periodic reviews of these systems are necessary to ensure they remain effective and efficient. This iterative approach to feedback integration helps keep the model current and responsive to new challenges and opportunities.

These lessons and practical advice underscore the dynamic and iterative nature of managing LLMs, highlighting the importance of adaptability and rigorous process management in achieving long-term success and relevance.

Summary

This chapter provided an extensive overview of monitoring LLMs, the integration of human feedback, and the continuous improvement processes for LLMOps. It began by exploring the fundamentals of monitoring, including metrics and monitoring tools, and illustrated these concepts through real-world case studies. The latter sections went into the critical role of human feedback in refining LLM outputs, detailing methods for its collection and integration, and culminating in a discussion on iterative processes that leverage feedback for ongoing enhancements, supported by success stories from industry leaders. In the next chapter, we'll cover the future direction of LLMs and their impacts on the AI space.

The Future of LLMOps and Emerging Technologies

We'll now review the current trends, technologies, and frameworks shaping LLMOps. This chapter reviews the dynamics of LLMOps, providing a comprehensive outlook on how these systems are developed, deployed, and managed responsibly. You will gain insights into the emerging technologies that are defining the next generation of language models and explore their benefits. By the end of this chapter, you will be equipped with the knowledge to understand and participate in the development of advanced LLM systems, while also being able to critically assess their implications and contribute to the discourse on responsible AI.

In this chapter, we're going to cover the following main topics:

- Identifying trends in LLM development

- Emerging technologies in LLMOps

- Considering responsible AI

- Developing talent and skill

- Planning and risk management

Identifying trends in LLM development

Let's first review several trends in the development of LLMs. This will set us up to later review the emerging technologies in terms of LLMOps.

Advancements in model architectures

The field of **large language models (LLMs)** has seen a definitive shift with the introduction of transformer models, which are fundamental to the advancements in the architecture of these models. Transformers, characterized by their attention mechanisms, allow models to weigh the importance of different words in a sentence, irrespective of their sequential order. This capability is useful in understanding complex patterns and relationships in data, making transformers good at handling tasks involving natural language understanding and generation.

The achievements of models such as ChatGPT, developed by OpenAI, and Llama-3 by Meta, have significantly pushed the boundaries of what LLMs can accomplish. With Llama-3 having 70B parameters, it showcases an ability to generate human-like text based on the prompts it receives. ChatGPT, on the other hand, with over 1 trillion parameters, enhances the way machines understand human language and has been widely adopted for tasks such as sentiment analysis, question answering, and data structuring.

Building upon these developments, newer architectures such as Switch Transformer have been introduced. Switch Transformer employs a sparsely activated technique – an alternate approach where only a subset of the model's parameters are activated for each specific task. This method allows the model to scale up dramatically in size — potentially to trillions of parameters — without a corresponding increase in computational demands during training. This technique is often referred to as **Mixture-of-Experts** or **MoE**. By only engaging relevant parts of the neural network, it optimizes processing efficiency and speeds up computation, making it feasible to train incredibly large models on existing hardware infrastructures.

Looking ahead, the trend in LLM architecture is moving toward even more modular and adaptable systems. Future architectures are anticipated to leverage the principles of **neural architecture search (NAS)**, a process that automates the design of neural networks. NAS could tailor architectures dynamically based on the specific characteristics of the dataset and the requirements of the task at hand. This means that models in the future might automatically configure themselves to best address the unique challenges posed by the data they are trained on, enhancing both performance and efficiency.

Such adaptable models would be highly specialized, designed to excel in particular domains or tasks by understanding the nuances and specific needs of the application. This could lead to more personalized and context-aware AI systems in fields ranging from healthcare, where models could predict patient outcomes and assist in diagnosis, to customer service, where they could understand and respond to customer queries with unprecedented accuracy.

Scaling models

Scaling LLMs presents both opportunities and challenges. As models scale, they generally improve in their understanding and generating capabilities, but they also require exponentially more computational power and data, which can be costly and resource intensive. Conversely, small language models offer a more resource-efficient alternative, though they may initially lack the sophistication of their larger counterparts. Strategies for scaling include more efficient data sampling techniques, the utilization of advanced hardware such as TPUs and custom GPU architectures, and techniques such as model distillation, which can be employed to reduce the size of large models and to enhance the capabilities of smaller models by transferring knowledge from larger models.

For example, OpenAI's GPT-3, which boasts 175 billion parameters, demonstrates the capabilities of scaled models in generating human-like text. At the other end of the spectrum, smaller models, such as Google's **Gemma**, offer a more manageable approach for applications with limited computational resources, showing that effective language understanding can still be achieved with as few as 2B parameters. Case studies, such as Google's Gemini model, used across Google Search, show how such technologies have been successfully implemented on a large scale, processing millions of queries with increased relevance in search results with smaller model requirements.

These implementations highlight the need for solutions to manage the cost and complexity of scaling and underscore the potential of smaller models in contexts where computational efficiency is key. The dual approach of employing both large and small models allows for a broader range of applications, accommodating various performance and resource requirements.

Integration of multimodal capabilities

The integration of multimodal capabilities into LLMs is rapidly advancing, starting a significant evolution in how these models interact with and interpret various data forms. As the internet becomes increasingly multimedia-rich, LLMs such as OpenAI's Sora and Google's multimodal Gemini are pioneering the fusion of visual and linguistic data. This capability is increasingly important, enhancing user interaction through more sophisticated AI applications, and has begun to broaden the scope of AI's utility across different sectors.

Beyond just text and images, the integration of stable diffusion techniques for image and video generation, and audio synthesis, further enhances the versatility of LLMs. Stable diffusion models enable the generation of high-quality, detailed images and videos from textual descriptions, offering vast potential for creative and design industries. For instance, these models can be used to automatically generate advertising content or assist in film production by creating realistic scenes and characters based on script descriptions.

Moreover, the addition of audio synthesis capabilities allows LLMs to produce human-like speech, music, or any sound effects from textual inputs, which can transform content creation within media and entertainment industries. This capability can be integrated into virtual assistants, making them interact in natural language while also responding with contextually appropriate sounds or music, providing a richer interaction experience.

These multimodal models are becoming incredibly adept at handling complex, mixed data types, thereby opening new avenues for AI applications. In healthcare, for example, models that can analyze and interpret medical imagery alongside clinical notes could revolutionize diagnostic processes by providing more accurate, comprehensive medical assessments without the need for extensive human intervention. Similarly, in education, these models can create interactive learning environments that adapt to the learning material by generating relevant images, videos, or audio explanations, thus catering to various learning styles and needs.

Furthermore, the integration of these technologies into LLMs supports the development of advanced content recommendation systems that understand user preferences not just based on text but also analyzing the visual and auditory content they consume. This results in more accurate and personalized content recommendations across platforms, enhancing user engagement and satisfaction.

As these technologies continue to improve, the potential for LLMs to operate as truly general AI systems becomes apparent, making them indispensable tools across virtually all sectors of society and industry. The challenge will be to ensure these models are developed ethically and responsibly, particularly as their capabilities and impact on everyday life continue to expand.

Efficiency improvements

Efficiency improvements are key for the sustainable growth of LLMs, particularly as the environmental impact of training such models becomes increasingly apparent. Techniques such as quantization, which reduces the precision of the numbers used in computations, and pruning, which eliminates unnecessary weights from a model, play significant roles in enhancing efficiency. Moreover, advances in both hardware and software continue to support more efficient model training and deployment, leading to reduced energy consumption and faster processing times.

NVIDIA's A100 GPUs, specifically designed for data centers, have already made significant strides in enhancing performance for AI workloads. They reduce the time and energy required for model training considerably. However, the recent introduction of the **NVIDIA H100 GPU** represents a further leap in efficiency. The H100 is built on the new **Hopper architecture**, which provides superior performance in handling AI-specific computations compared to the A100, making it even more suitable for training complex LLMs.

Additionally, the development of **Application-Specific Integrated Circuits (ASICs)** and dedicated LLM chips is altering the landscape. These specialized chips are tailored specifically to optimize machine learning tasks, offering higher efficiency and lower power consumption compared to general-purpose GPUs. This specialization boosts processing speeds, all while cutting down the operational costs associated with training and running LLMs.

The impact of these technological advancements is evident in the decreasing cost of training large models. For instance, OpenAI's GPT-3, which was initially estimated to cost around $60 million to train, has paved the way for new models that can be trained for single-digit millions today. This drastic reduction in costs is largely due to more efficient hardware solutions such as the H100 and specialized ASICs, as well as improvements in model training algorithms and compression techniques.

Software solutions also contribute significantly to this efficiency drive. Model compression algorithms, for example, make it feasible to deploy state-of-the-art LLMs on a variety of platforms, including mobile devices, by significantly reducing the model size while maintaining performance. This capability enables on-device AI applications that were previously not feasible due to the limited processing power and storage capacity of mobile hardware.

Together, these trends show an advancing field and highlight the broadening scope of applications and the continuous need for novel solutions to harness the full potential of LLMs efficiently and ethically. As technology advances, it opens new possibilities for deploying powerful AI models more broadly, ensuring that the benefits of AI can be realized across industries in an environmentally sustainable and cost-effective manner.

Let's now dive into emerging technologies in LLMOps.

Emerging technologies in LLMOps

The following technologies are being iterated and perfected to address the technological advancements that come with LLM developments.

Automated Machine Learning (AutoML)

Automated Machine Learning (AutoML) is improving the development and tuning of LLMs by streamlining model selection, composition, and parameterization. This technology significantly accelerates the development cycle of LLMs, allowing developers to reduce the time spent on iterative tuning and focus more on strategic aspects of model deployment. AutoML enables even those without deep expertise in data science to develop competitive models, effectively democratizing advanced AI capabilities across various sectors.

Integration of AutoGPT and Distilabel in AutoML

Recent advancements such as AutoGPT extend the capabilities of AutoML specifically within the field of generative pre-trained transformers. AutoGPT automates the process of generating LLMs tailored for specific use cases. This automation is particularly beneficial in scenarios requiring rapid deployment of customized solutions across different domains, from customer service to personalized content creation. By automating the initial setup and tuning of GPT models, AutoGPT reduces the barrier to entry for organizations looking to leverage state-of-the-art language processing for niche applications.

Similarly, **Distilabel**, another tool, harnesses AutoML to streamline the creation of training datasets. It utilizes a combination of active learning and model distillation to generate synthetic data that can effectively train LLMs. This approach enhances the efficiency of the data generation process and also addresses common data constraints such as limited labeled datasets in specific domains. By producing high-quality synthetic data, Distilabel allows for the continuous improvement of models even in the absence of extensive real-world data.

Benefits of AutoML in operational settings

The primary advantage of integrating tools such as AutoGPT and Distilabel into AutoML workflows is the dramatic reduction in development time and resources required to produce effective LLMs. Companies can deploy specialized models more quickly, enabling faster responses to market changes and user needs. Additionally, AutoML's capacity to handle routine data processing and model adjustments frees up human experts to tackle more complex problems, adding strategic value.

Challenges and limitations

Despite these benefits, the deployment of AutoML in highly specialized domains presents several challenges. The nuanced understanding required in fields such as legal or medical services may exceed the current capabilities of AutoML systems. In these cases, the lack of custom settings and potential issues with model transparency and explainability become significant. For instance, models automatically generated by AutoGPT might not fully align with the intricate requirements or ethical considerations of specific industries without human oversight.

Moreover, the risk of models overfitting or underfitting is heightened when they are auto-generated. The synthetic data produced by tools such as Distilabel, while useful, must be meticulously verified for accuracy and relevance to prevent the reinforcement of biases or errors during training. Ensuring the quality and applicability of synthetic data is required for maintaining the integrity and performance of the resulting models.

Looking forward, the integration of AutoML into LLM development is likely to expand, driven by the growing need for personalized and highly specific AI solutions across industries. Enhancements in AutoML tools will focus on improving the sophistication of automatically generated models and the quality of synthetic data, aiming to match – and eventually surpass – the effectiveness of manually tuned models. As these technologies mature, they promise to enhance the accessibility and efficiency of AI and to change how industries operate by leveraging automated, intelligent systems.

Federated learning

Federated learning is an approach to training LLMs that adapts to a wide array of computational environments, from smartphones to server-grade machines. This approach is important for accommodating the diversity in model size and complexity, ensuring that systems are inclusive of both large-scale models and smaller, localized models. The key to this inclusivity lies in designing federated systems capable of integrating multiple types of devices, each contributing uniquely to the model's learning process. It's vital to ensure that contributions from smaller models are valued just as much as those from larger models, preventing any overshadowing and promoting a truly collaborative learning environment.

To enhance the efficiency of federated LLMs, adopting parameter-efficient training methods is essential. Techniques such as transfer learning and model pruning help reduce the number of parameters that need to be actively trained, thereby minimizing the computational demand on individual devices and speeding up the overall training process. By using a pre-trained model and fine-tuning it locally on devices, the need for extensive computation and data transmission across the network can be significantly reduced, streamlining the training process without compromising the model's effectiveness.

Another cornerstone of federated learning is the protection of intellectual property through **FedIPR (Federated Intellectual Property Rights)**. This initiative involves implementing encryption protocols and secure aggregation techniques to shield the unique characteristics of the LLMs being trained. By safeguarding the proprietary aspects of these models, FedIPR ensures that the competitive edge of the industry remains intact and that participants cannot reverse engineer key features.

Ensuring data privacy during both training and inference phases is also important. Techniques such as differential privacy, which introduces noise to obscure individual data contributions, and homomorphic encryption, allowing computations on encrypted data, are fundamental in a federated learning context. These privacy-preserving mechanisms are critical for maintaining data security, ensuring that even if data or model updates are intercepted during transmission, they remain unintelligible and secure.

Together, these design principles define a robust framework for federated learning, aiming to foster efficient, secure, and collaborative training environments. They ensure that federated LLMs perform optimally and adhere to stringent privacy and intellectual property standards, making this approach suitable for a variety of applications across numerous privacy-sensitive industries.

Implementing these design principles in federated learning involves addressing several key challenges. Coordinating updates across diverse and distributed datasets requires sophisticated synchronization and communication protocols to ensure data integrity and consistency. Additionally, balancing the trade-offs between model accuracy and privacy, especially when employing techniques such as differential privacy, involves careful tuning to prevent significant degradation in model performance.

Moreover, the variability in data quality and representativeness across different nodes can affect the overall model's effectiveness. Strategies such as weighted aggregation, where updates from more reliable or representative nodes are given greater importance, can help mitigate this issue.

As federated learning continues to evolve, these principles and strategies will play a critical role in enabling the secure, efficient, and effective training of LLMs across decentralized environments. By adhering to these principles, federated learning can improve the landscape of data privacy and model training, opening new possibilities for deploying advanced AI solutions in sensitive and regulatory-bound industries.

Edge computing

Edge computing represents a paradigm shift in how data is processed, moving much of the workload to the periphery of the network, closer to where data originates. This approach is especially pertinent for applications that demand immediate processing speeds and stringent privacy controls, such as real-time language translation devices, autonomous vehicles, and predictive maintenance systems in manufacturing settings. By processing data locally, edge computing facilitates rapid response times and minimizes the latency that can hamper applications reliant on near-instantaneous feedback. Additionally, local data processing helps reduce bandwidth costs and network congestion, as less data needs to be sent to and from a centralized cloud or data center.

The integration of LLMs into edge computing frameworks enables sophisticated AI capabilities such as natural language understanding and decision-making to be executed directly on edge devices. This capability is crucial for scenarios such as autonomous vehicles, which must process and react to vast amounts of sensory data in real time to make driving decisions, or for IoT devices that operate in remote locations where connectivity might be sporadic or unreliable.

However, deploying LLMs at the edge is not without its challenges. Edge devices often have limited computational power, storage, and energy resources compared to traditional data center environments. This limitation necessitates the development of lighter, more efficient versions of LLMs that can operate within the constraints of edge hardware without a significant loss in performance. Techniques such as model pruning, quantization, and knowledge distillation are commonly employed to reduce the size and computational demands of these models while maintaining their effectiveness.

Furthermore, managing and updating LLMs across numerous edge nodes introduces complexities in version control and data consistency. Ensuring that each device is running the most current model iteration and has not been compromised in terms of data integrity or security is a non-trivial task that requires robust, automated systems. Solutions for these issues include the use of federated learning, where model updates are collaboratively trained across multiple edge devices and only the model updates are transmitted, rather than raw data, thereby maintaining privacy and reducing data transmission requirements.

Moreover, to effectively leverage edge computing capabilities, there is a growing trend toward deploying advanced edge devices equipped with specialized AI processing chips. These chips are designed to perform machine learning tasks more efficiently, allowing even complex LLMs to be run on the edge. Companies are increasingly investing in these technologies to enable smarter, autonomous systems that can operate independently of central servers, making real-time AI a reality across a range of industries.

AI and IoT convergence

The integration of **artificial intelligence (AI)** and the **Internet of Things (IoT)** marks a significant advancement in technology, fostering environments that are not only smarter but highly interconnected too. As LLMs merge with IoT data streams, they unlock powerful capabilities for real-time data processing and analysis, which are critical for advanced decision-making and automation across various sectors.

In smart cities, for example, the convergence of AI and IoT allows for the dynamic management of urban infrastructure. IoT devices installed throughout a city, from traffic lights to sensors on public transit systems, can collect vast amounts of data on traffic patterns and public transport usage. When this data is analyzed in real time by LLMs, it enables city planners to make immediate adjustments to traffic light sequences and public transport schedules, optimizing traffic flow and reducing congestion. Similarly, AI can help in predictive maintenance of urban infrastructure, where sensors detect potential faults in utilities, and AI systems quickly analyze this data to predict when and where maintenance work is needed.

In the healthcare sector, wearable devices and embedded sensors provide continuous monitoring of patient health metrics. When coupled with LLMs, these devices can process and interpret complex health data in real time, offering personalized treatment recommendations and alerting healthcare providers to potential health issues before they become critical. This real-time data processing can be lifesaving in emergency scenarios and significantly enhances ongoing patient care management.

Industrial applications also benefit greatly from AI-IoT integration. In manufacturing, sensors can track the status of equipment and environmental conditions, with LLMs analyzing this data to predict equipment failures before they occur. This predictive maintenance saves significant costs and downtime by allowing businesses to address mechanical issues proactively. Additionally, AI-enhanced IoT systems can optimize production processes by continually adjusting operational parameters for maximum efficiency and product quality.

Despite these advantages, the integration of AI and IoT presents several challenges that must be addressed to realize its full potential. One major challenge is the seamless integration of heterogeneous devices and data formats. IoT ecosystems often involve various devices with different operating standards and communication protocols, making it difficult to create a unified system where data can be easily shared and analyzed.

Moreover, the sheer volume of data generated by countless IoT devices poses significant challenges in data management and analysis. Processing this data effectively requires robust, scalable AI systems capable of handling large datasets quickly and efficiently. Additionally, as data flows continuously from diverse sources, maintaining data integrity and timeliness becomes crucial.

Security is another critical concern. With data being transmitted across multiple nodes in an IoT network, ensuring the security and privacy of this data against cyber threats is critical. Robust encryption methods, secure data transmission protocols, and continuous security monitoring are essential to protect sensitive information and maintain trust in IoT systems.

Addressing these challenges requires ongoing iteration in both AI and IoT technologies. As solutions evolve, the convergence of AI and IoT is set to revolutionize how we interact with and manage the technology in our environments, making systems smarter, more responsive, and more efficient.

Considering responsible AI

In terms of LLMs, transparency and explainability are paramount to building trust and ensuring accountability. The complex nature of these models often results in a **black box** scenario where the decision-making process is opaque and difficult for users to understand. Enhancing the explainability of LLM decisions involves several techniques, including the development of interpretable models and the integration of explanation interfaces.

One effective approach is the use of model-agnostic methods, such as **Local Interpretable Model-Agnostic Explanations (LIME)** and **SHapley Additive exPlanations (SHAP)**, which provide insights into how different features influence the output of any machine learning model, regardless of its complexity. These tools can help demystify LLM behaviors by indicating which parts of input data are most influential in determining the output.

Moreover, embedding explainability into the model architecture itself, such as through attention mechanisms that can highlight the parts of the input data most attended to by the model, provides a more natural and integrated approach to understanding model decisions. This level of transparency is crucial for user trust and regulatory compliance too. As governments and regulatory bodies increasingly demand clearer explanations of AI decision-making processes, ensuring that LLMs can provide comprehensible and accurate explanations of their actions becomes essential.

Privacy and data security

Privacy and data security are critical challenges in the training and deployment of LLMs, especially given the vast amounts of data they process. Ensuring the privacy of this data involves a multi-faceted approach, encompassing both technological solutions and strict governance protocols.

Technologically, techniques such as differential privacy introduce randomness into the datasets used for training LLMs, ensuring that the models cannot inadvertently leak personal information. Homomorphic encryption is another promising technology, allowing data to be processed in an encrypted form, providing results without ever exposing the underlying data.

Moreover, federated learning can be utilized to train models on decentralized data, which remains on local servers or devices and prevents the need to share sensitive information centrally. However, these technologies must be complemented with robust data governance policies that dictate clear guidelines on data usage, access controls, and audit trails, ensuring that all data handling adheres to privacy laws and ethical standards.

Regulatory compliance

The rapid advancement and integration of LLMs into various sectors have caught the attention of regulators worldwide, leading to an evolving landscape of AI-specific regulations. Staying compliant with these regulations requires a proactive approach, understanding current laws, and anticipating future legal trends.

Globally, frameworks such as the European Union's **General Data Protection Regulation (GDPR)** and the **California Consumer Privacy Act (CCPA)** in the U.S. set strict guidelines on data privacy, requiring companies to ensure transparency and user control over personal data. More recently, the EU's proposed **Artificial Intelligence Act** is looking to impose additional requirements specifically tailored to AI systems, classifying them based on their risk levels and imposing stricter compliance requirements on high-risk applications.

Strategies for compliance include the implementation of comprehensive AI governance frameworks that ensure all aspects of LLM deployment, from data collection to model decisions, are in line with legal requirements. Regular audits, both internal and external, are central to verifying compliance and identifying potential areas of risk. Additionally, maintaining agility in regulatory compliance – being able to adapt quickly to new laws and guidelines – is essential for organizations that utilize LLMs to avoid penalties and legal challenges.

Together, these pages outline the ethical landscape that surrounds the deployment of large language models. By addressing transparency, privacy, and regulatory compliance, organizations can ensure that their use of LLMs adheres to ethical standards and legal requirements, fostering trust and enabling responsible development and use of AI technologies.

Preparing for next-generation LLMs

Focus needs to be placed on building adaptive and flexible LLMOps frameworks. It's essential that organizations adopt a forward-thinking mindset. Modular architectures, for instance, offer the agility needed to swap in and out components or services as required without disrupting the overall system functionality. This flexibility is crucial for integrating advancements in machine learning and data processing that can significantly improve the performance and capabilities of LLMs. By designing systems that are inherently adaptable, organizations can avoid the pitfalls of obsolescence and ensure that their operations are always at the cutting edge.

Open standards and APIs play a pivotal role in this ecosystem by promoting interoperability and reducing the complexity associated with adopting new technologies. They allow different systems and components to communicate seamlessly, reducing integration times and enabling more straightforward upgrades or enhancements. This openness supports technical agility and fosters a broader community of innovators, where developers and companies can contribute to and benefit from shared advancements.

Furthermore, the integration of automation and AI-driven analytics into LLMOps frameworks dramatically enhances operational efficiency. By automating routine tasks and using AI to analyze operational data, organizations can identify inefficiencies and optimize processes in real time. This capability is particularly valuable in environments where LLMs must process vast amounts of data or make decisions quickly. Automation also helps in scaling operations effectively by minimizing the need for manual intervention and allowing staff to focus on more strategic tasks.

The use of predictive analytics and machine learning within these frameworks can anticipate future challenges and opportunities. For example, predictive maintenance can foresee potential issues in data centers that host LLMs, enabling proactive repairs that prevent downtime. Similarly, machine learning algorithms can analyze user interaction data to predict shifts in user behavior, providing insights that help refine and personalize the LLM's responses.

Ultimately, the ability to adapt to and integrate new technologies rapidly is what will differentiate leading organizations that leverage LLMs. Those that invest in creating flexible, responsive, and intelligent operational frameworks are well placed to leverage the full potential of LLM advancements, driving change within their organizations and across the entire industry. This strategic approach enhances competitive advantage and contributes to the broader development of ethical and effective AI technologies.

Infrastructure and resource planning

As the complexity and data demands of LLMs escalate, the infrastructure underpinning these systems must keep pace and also proactively anticipate future needs. This requires a generic strategy for developing computational and infrastructure resources that are robust, scalable, and efficient, ensuring they can support the evolving requirements of advanced LLMs.

Managing the operational costs and environmental impacts of running high-performance LLMs is key. Incorporating advanced data center technologies such as liquid cooling systems can drastically reduce the heat generated by servers, thus lowering the energy required for cooling. Liquid cooling, more efficient than traditional air cooling, is becoming vital in data centers engaged in intensive computations. Additionally, employing energy-efficient processors helps to cut down power consumption and reduce the overall carbon footprint of these data centers, aligning with broader sustainability goals.

Beyond physical hardware optimizations, software solutions such as workload orchestration and resource virtualization are critical for enhancing operational efficiency. Workload orchestration tools dynamically allocate resources according to real-time demand, optimizing the use of computational power. Virtualization technology, on the other hand, facilitates the creation of multiple simulated environments from a single physical system, maximizing the utility of existing infrastructure while minimizing the need for new hardware investments.

Scalability and flexibility

The scalability necessary for next-generation LLMs requires infrastructure solutions that can swiftly adapt to changing demands. Cloud-based solutions excel in this area, offering scalable and flexible resources without the hefty initial capital outlay required by traditional on-premise setups. These services allow organizations to easily scale resources up or down based on operational needs, ensuring efficiency even during fluctuating workload periods.

Investments in specialized AI chips and high-performance computing systems are also vital. These technologies are tailored to manage the specific workloads of state-of-the-art LLMs, providing faster processing times and reduced latency, which are essential for complex AI computations.

Redundancy and disaster recovery

Comprehensive infrastructure planning also encompasses strategies for redundancy and disaster recovery to ensure data integrity and system availability. Implementing redundant systems and regular backups safeguards against data loss due to hardware malfunctions, natural disasters, or cyber-attacks. Additionally, strategies such as geographically distributed data centers and real-time data replication across sites are required for maintaining operations during unforeseen disruptions, ensuring that backup data is continuously updated and secured.

Future-proofing infrastructure investments

Looking ahead, organizations must future-proof their infrastructure investments by considering current technological requirements and projected advancements in AI and computing. Collaborating with technology forecasters and investing in modular, upgradeable systems can position organizations to rapidly adapt to new technologies as they emerge.

By addressing these key areas – efficiency, scalability, flexibility, redundancy, and future-proofing, organizations can forge a robust infrastructure strategy that supports both the present and future demands of deploying and managing sophisticated large language models. This strategic approach meets operational requirements that then drive and support long-term growth in the dynamic field of AI.

Developing talent and skill

As LLM technology continues to advance, the demand for specialized skill sets extends beyond traditional boundaries of AI and machine learning into areas that require a combination of technical acumen and interdisciplinary expertise. The evolving landscape of LLMs necessitates roles such as synthetic data generation specialists, prompt engineers, and policy optimizers, each contributing uniquely to the development and implementation of these sophisticated systems.

As data privacy concerns and the availability of large-scale training datasets continue to pose challenges, the role of synthetic data generation specialists becomes increasingly critical. These professionals are tasked with designing methods to generate artificial data that can safely and effectively train LLMs without compromising real data's integrity or privacy. This role requires a deep understanding of both machine learning algorithms and data privacy laws, ensuring that synthetic data is diverse, representative, and compliant with regulatory standards.

The effectiveness of an LLM often hinges on the quality of the prompts it receives, making the role of prompt engineers vital. These individuals specialize in crafting prompts that maximize the performance of LLMs, requiring both creative linguistic flair and a technical understanding of model architecture. Prompt engineers work to understand the nuances of language models and develop prompts that can effectively guide the models to produce desired outcomes, enhancing the utility and accuracy of their responses.

As LLMs become integrated into more critical applications, the need for policy optimizers grows. These professionals develop strategies to align model outputs with ethical guidelines and regulatory requirements. Their work ensures that LLMs operate within set boundaries and adhere to societal norms and values, which is important in sectors such as healthcare, finance, and public services. Policy optimizers must balance technical knowledge with an understanding of ethics, law, and social impact, crafting guidelines that help models navigate complex moral landscapes.

To cultivate these advanced skills, organizations need to implement comprehensive training and development strategies. Customized learning pathways are essential, allowing employees to focus on acquiring specific competencies related to their roles. For example, training programs for synthetic data specialists might focus on data anonymization techniques and the latest advancements in data simulation technologies, while prompt engineers might receive specialized training in linguistics and user experience design.

Partnering with academic institutions to develop specialized curricula and certification programs can also provide the workforce with cutting-edge knowledge and formal qualifications. These partnerships can be instrumental in keeping the curriculum relevant to the latest industry requirements and technological advancements.

Furthermore, fostering a culture of continuous professional development and lifelong learning is required to keep the workforce agile and prepared to adapt to new challenges and iterate on LLM technology. Encouraging participation in workshops, webinars, and conferences, as well as providing access to online courses and resources, can help maintain a skilled, knowledgeable, and motivated team capable of driving forward the capabilities of LLM technology.

By embracing these strategies and recognizing the importance of these emerging roles, organizations can ensure their teams are equipped to handle the current demands of LLM operations and are also poised to lead future developments in this field.

Collaboration and partnership

Collaboration and partnership are indispensable strategies for fostering industry growth and pushing the boundaries of LLM technology. As these models become increasingly integral to a wide array of applications – from customer service automation to advanced predictive analytics, the need for diverse insights and expertise becomes more apparent. Engaging in strategic partnerships with tech giants, start-ups, and research-focused academic institutions opens doors to a wealth of knowledge, resources, and cutting-edge technologies that might otherwise be inaccessible.

Partnering with established tech giants often provides access to vast infrastructure resources, advanced research and development tools, and a deep pool of expertise that can significantly accelerate the pace of LLM development. These collaborations can take various forms, including joint research projects, shared labs, and technology exchange programs. For start-ups and smaller enterprises, such partnerships are particularly beneficial, offering a faster route to scaling their technologies and integrating industry-leading practices and standards into their operations.

Conversely, collaborations with start-ups can be equally advantageous for larger corporations. Start-ups often bring innovative approaches and nimble technologies to the table, driving larger companies to explore new ideas and adopt more agile methodologies. These partnerships might involve incubator or accelerator programs where larger firms support start-ups through funding, mentoring, and providing technical support, fostering an environment where new ideas can thrive and be tested at scale.

Academic institutions are key in advancing the foundational science behind LLMs. Collaborations with universities can involve setting up sponsored research, establishing scholarships, or creating co-op programs that allow students and researchers to work directly on real-world applications. These partnerships help ensure that the theoretical advancements in machine learning and artificial intelligence are continuously translated into practical, applicable solutions. Moreover, such engagements help prepare the next generation of AI professionals, equipped with the latest knowledge and skills tailored to the needs of the industry.

Building ecosystems from scratch extends beyond forming individual partnerships to creating networks that connect multiple stakeholders, including companies, academic institutions, government agencies, and non-governmental organizations. These ecosystems facilitate a multidirectional flow of ideas and resources, ensuring that industry contributions are refined and implemented at a pace that individual efforts cannot match.

To successfully manage these ecosystems, it is imperative to establish platforms that support seamless communication and collaboration. Digital collaboration tools, shared data repositories, and regular networking events can help maintain the momentum of these cooperative efforts. Clear agreements on intellectual property, a transparent approach to data sharing, and mutually agreed-upon goals are essential to align the interests of all parties and maximize the outcomes of collaborative efforts.

For collaborations to be successful, they must be managed with a clear framework that defines roles, responsibilities, and expectations. Regular reviews and adjustments to the collaborative agreements can help address any challenges and align efforts with evolving objectives and market conditions. Recognizing and celebrating shared successes motivates continued cooperation to eventually highlight the tangible benefits of these partnerships, encouraging further investment and engagement from all stakeholders.

Planning and risk management

Scenario planning and risk management are essential for organizations that aim to leverage LLMs effectively while navigating the complexities and uncertainties inherent in rapidly advancing technologies. These strategies enable organizations to prepare for various potential futures, optimizing their readiness for both the opportunities and challenges that next-generation LLMs may present.

Scenario planning involves constructing detailed, plausible scenarios that cover a spectrum of possible future states, from the most optimistic outcomes to potential crises or challenges. This process starts with identifying key drivers of change in the LLM landscape, such as technological breakthroughs, regulatory changes, or shifts in market demand. Organizations then develop scenarios that illustrate how these drivers could affect their operations and strategic goals. For instance, a best-case scenario might depict a market where new LLM technologies provide a significant competitive advantage, leading to increased market share and revenue. Conversely, a worst-case scenario could involve regulatory changes that restrict the use of LLMs, requiring rapid adaptation and possible restructuring of operations.

By exploring these scenarios, organizations can better understand potential risks and opportunities, enabling them to develop flexible strategies that remain robust across different futures. Scenario planning also aids in the development of early warning systems that can alert organizations to signs that a particular scenario may be unfolding, allowing them to adjust their strategies proactively.

Effective risk management for LLM deployments involves identifying potential risks, assessing their likelihood and potential impact, and developing strategies to mitigate these risks before they manifest as serious issues. Key risks include technological failures, such as software bugs or hardware malfunctions, that could lead to downtime or incorrect model outputs. Data breaches represent another critical risk, particularly given the sensitive nature of the data often processed by LLMs.

To manage these risks, organizations should implement comprehensive risk assessments that regularly evaluate the vulnerability of their LLM systems. This involves both technical assessments to ensure the integrity and security of the systems and process evaluations to ensure that operational practices do not inadvertently increase risk. Continuous monitoring systems play a critical role here, utilizing advanced analytics to detect anomalies that could indicate potential failures or security breaches.

Contingency planning is another major element of risk management. Organizations must develop and maintain robust contingency plans that can be activated in the event of a failure or breach. These plans should include procedures for rapidly isolating affected systems, communicating with stakeholders, and switching to backup systems if necessary. Training and regular drills for key personnel ensure that everyone knows their roles during an incident, which is critical for effective response and minimizing downtime or damage.

Integrating scenario planning with risk management allows organizations to prepare not just for likely risks but also for extreme events that could have high impacts. This integrated approach ensures that organizations remain agile and can respond to both expected challenges and those that arise from unforeseen changes in the technological, regulatory, or economic environment.

Together, these strategies equip organizations to handle upcoming technological shifts and position them to lead improvements in the field of LLMs. By preparing for a range of potential futures and developing robust risk management protocols, organizations can navigate the evolving landscape with confidence, ensuring both operational continuity and strategic advantage.

Summary

This final chapter explored the changing landscape of **large language model operations (LLMOps)**, highlighting key emerging trends, technological advancements, and the importance of ethical practices in the development and application of LLMs. It reviewed the challenges that accompany these powerful technologies, advocating for responsible AI and the implementation of ethical guidelines. Additionally, the chapter discussed strategic preparations for next-generation language models, emphasizing the need for organizations to stay adaptable and forward-thinking to harness the full potential of LLMs effectively.

Index

www.packtpub.com

Subscribe to our online digital library for full access to over 7,000 books and videos, as well as industry leading tools to help you plan your personal development and advance your career. For more information, please visit our website.

Why subscribe?

- Spend less time learning and more time coding with practical eBooks and Videos from over 4,000 industry professionals

- Improve your learning with Skill Plans built especially for you

- Get a free eBook or video every month

- Fully searchable for easy access to vital information

- Copy and paste, print, and bookmark content

Did you know that Packt offers eBook versions of every book published, with PDF and ePub files available? You can upgrade to the eBook version at packtpub.com and as a print book customer, you are entitled to a discount on the eBook copy. Get in touch with us at customercare@packtpub.com for more details.

At www.packtpub.com, you can also read a collection of free technical articles, sign up for a range of free newsletters, and receive exclusive discounts and offers on Packt books and eBooks.

Other Books You May Enjoy

If you enjoyed this book, you may be interested in these other books by Packt:

OpenAI API Cookbook

Henry Habib

ISBN: 978-1-80512-135-0

- Grasp the fundamentals of the OpenAI API

- Navigate the API's capabilities and limitations of the API

- Set up the OpenAI API with step-by-step instructions, from obtaining your API key to making your first call

- Explore advanced features such as system messages, fine-tuning, and the effects of different parameters

- Integrate the OpenAI API into existing applications and workflows to enhance their functionality with AI

- Design and build applications that fully harness the power of ChatGPT

Mastering NLP from Foundations to LLMs

Lior Gazit, Meysam Ghaffari

ISBN: 978-1-80461-918-6

- Master the mathematical foundations of machine learning and NLP

- Implement advanced techniques for preprocessing text data and analysis

- Design ML-NLP systems in Python

- Model and classify text using traditional machine learning and deep learning methods

- Understand the theory and design of LLMs and their implementation for various applications in AI

- Explore NLP insights, trends, and expert opinions on its future direction and potential

Packt is searching for authors like you

If you're interested in becoming an author for Packt, please visit `authors.packtpub.com` and apply today. We have worked with thousands of developers and tech professionals, just like you, to help them share their insight with the global tech community. You can make a general application, apply for a specific hot topic that we are recruiting an author for, or submit your own idea.

Share Your Thoughts

Now you've finished *Essential Guide to LLMOps*, we'd love to hear your thoughts! Scan the QR code below to go straight to the Amazon review page for this book and share your feedback or leave a review on the site that you purchased it from.

`https://packt.link/r/1-835-88751-1`

Your review is important to us and the tech community and will help us make sure we're delivering excellent quality content.